PREHISTORIC ANIMALS

PREHISTORIC

by Sam and Beryl Epstein

pictures by W. R. Lohse

FRANKLIN WATTS, INCORPORATED

NEW YORK

ANIMALS

The authors wish to express their thanks to Mrs. Mary B. Patsuris and Dr. Bobb Schaeffer of the Department of Geology and Paleontology, The American Museum of Natural History, New York, for their invaluable help and the many suggestions they contributed to the writing of this book.

contents

illustrations

Table

PREHISTORIC ANIMALS

1 *clues and detectives*

THE STORY OF PREHISTORIC ANIMALS IS IN REALITY TWO stories.

One of these stories is that of the strange and varied animals who lived in the dim past, long before recorded history.

The other story is the fascinating answer to a question: How do we know about these animals, many of them extinct, who lived so long ago?

This second story is really a sort of detective story, in which many people have worked together, trying to solve a mystery. The story tells, first of all, how people learned that there was a mystery to be solved—how they came to guess that strange animals had inhabited the earth ages before man himself existed.

For a long time, nobody did guess that there was a mystery. Everybody took for granted that the animals they saw around them were the same varieties that had always inhabited the world, since the beginning of time. Once in a

while, to be sure, men accidentally found rocks on which
there seemed to be the unfamiliar imprint of a leaf or a
shell, or in which stony shapes that looked like strange
bones seemed to be embedded. Usually they called these
curiosities "freaks of nature." They thought they were
stones that just happened to be formed in odd ways.

But a few people puzzled over the rocks and wondered
if there might not possibly be another explanation for
them.

About 2,500 years ago, a few Greek thinkers voiced
their suspicion that the odd forms in the rocks were clues
to a strange and mysterious world of animals that had
existed at some time in the past. But almost nobody believed these men. Most people found it impossible to understand that the natural world around them might ever
have been different from the one they knew.

But gradually the clues piled up, and more and more
people became curious about the evidence, and the mystery at which it hinted. Finally, about 150 years ago,
various scientifically minded people determined to collect
as many clues as possible, study them carefully, and solve
the mystery which lay behind them. They were the
founders of the science of paleontology, which means "the
study of ancient life."

The scientists who work in this field are called paleontologists. The clues they collect are called fossils, a name
that somewhat explains itself. The word fossil comes from
the Latin word which means "to dig," and a fossil is
usually dug up out of the earth, although sometimes it is
found on the surface. It may be a perfectly preserved bone,
or a bone in which cells have been replaced by a mineral

substance, so that the bone has become petrified. It may be a footprint made in wet mud that later hardened and turned to rock, so that the print was preserved like the paw mark of a dog made in wet concrete. It may be the impression of a fish or a leaf, originally made in soft lava or soft clay that later turned to stone. Or it may be simply a shape, or mold, of one of these things, formed when the body of some soft creature—a worm, for example—decayed after it had been covered with mud. The worm-shaped tube, left in the mud, might then have filled with sand or earth. This sand or earth filling, which took the exact shape of the worm, became a fossil called a "worm cast."

Today paleontologists work closely with another group of scientists, the geologists, who study the ancient history of the earth itself—the formation of its mountains and valleys, its continents and seas. Together these two groups of scientists are coming closer and closer to a solution of the mystery of ancient life on our planet. Some of them work in museum or college laboratories, some in the laboratories of industrial organizations. Some endure bitterly cold winds or hot desert suns as they dig patiently down through layers of rock to collect clues that have lain buried for millions of years.

The mystery of ancient life is still not completely solved, but more of it is becoming clear every day. For example, scientists have worked out a theory that, more than three billion years ago, the earth may possibly have been formed as a whirling ball of hot gases torn from the sun. They believe that the gases on the surface of the ball may have slowly cooled and turned to liquid rock, and that this liquid finally hardened into a rough solid crust. They also believe that at many times in the long history of the earth this crust has heaved up into mountains, and that centuries of rain and wind have worn each new group of mountains down again. They call this wearing-down process "erosion," and they know that erosion always results in heavy layers of sediment, which has been carried down the earth's slopes into valleys or into the sea.

The scientists believe that some kind of life first appeared on the earth about two billion years ago, by a process they still do not understand. They only know that chemical substances combined into units that somehow had the ability to reproduce themselves. Probably these first units were merely tiny jellylike blobs, so soft that they left no clues behind for scientists to study.

The earliest definite clues the scientists have found came, they think, from a time over five hundred million years ago. Those clues, of course, are fossils, and they were found in certain layers of sediment which the scientists believe must have been forming at the time the fossil creatures were living. Scientists still know comparatively little about the earliest creatures who lived on the earth. They are certain, however, that they all made their home in the sea, and that they were invertebrates: animals without backbones. The ancient time during which they were the earth's only living animals is sometimes called the Age of Invertebrates.

2 the mystery of the rocks

IN STUDYING THE HISTORY OF THE EARTH, SCIENTISTS HAVE been able to estimate its approximate age, and they have divided that age up into time divisions, each with a distinguishing name. There is a story behind these divisions and names.

One of the outstanding characters in the story was a man named William Smith, who was born in England in 1769. People knew very little about fossils at that time. The science of paleontology, or the study of ancient life, didn't even exist. But before Smith's death it had become a real and important science, and Smith was one of those who helped bring it into being.

William Smith was brought up on his uncle's farm. He didn't have a very cheerful time there, because he was always being scolded. His uncle thought the boy was lazy and useless, because William was never very helpful in the fields and around the barn. The only thing William really enjoyed doing was collecting stones and trying to answer his own questions about them.

When William was eighteen years old he found a job that suited him very well; he became a surveyor's assistant. Then nobody blamed him for studying the shape and location of rocks, because that was part of a surveyor's work.

As young Smith wandered back and forth over the countryside with his instruments, and especially as he watched men dig the Somerset coal canal he had helped to map out, he noticed all sorts of things. He noticed, for example, that most rocks were in layers, one on top of another, and he learned that those layers were called strata. Sometimes the strata were flat; sometimes they lifted in a curve, or tilted upward in a slant. He also noticed that some of the layers contained shells packed in the stone like raisins in a cake. Other layers seemed to be made entirely of tiny shells pressed close together. After a while Smith worked out an idea about those shells.

He reasoned like this. A particular kind of shell (let's call it X) was found in a stratum of blue limestone. X must have been alive when limy mud was being deposited, at a time when this part of England was flooded by the sea. The X shells must have lived and died on the sea floor, and, with other shells, packed together in the mud to form, later, this layer of limestone. There were never any X shells in the layer of rock under this limestone, or in the one on top of it, so probably the only time the X creatures were alive was at the time this one stratum was being formed.

Not long afterward Smith's work took him to another part of the country, where he found no blue limestone at all. But there was another kind of limestone at that place, of a grayish color, and it too contained X shells.

Smith guessed that this gray limestone was being formed at the same time as the blue limestone—at the time when the X creatures were alive. If he found these same shells in a limestone layer in some other part of England, he thought, he would know that layer had been formed at the same time too.

Many people made a hobby of collecting fossils in those days, and some of them had become quite certain that fossils were clues to the past. But they didn't know how to interpret them. They jumbled all sorts of fossils together on the shelves of museums, and were unable to tell whether all the creatures had lived at the same time or whether some had lived at one period and some at another. Usually, if they found a fossil close to the surface of the ground, they thought it was probably a clue to some animal that had lived quite recently. And if they found a fossil far below the surface, they took for granted it was that of an animal that had lived very long ago.

And then William Smith showed them a way to "date" their fossils.

He drew cross-section diagrams of the rock strata in different parts of England. Each diagram looked like a drawing of the inside of a layer cake after a slice has been cut off. And on each diagram Smith labeled the layer where he had found X shells, so that people would know that all those layers had been formed at the same time, whether they were close to the surface or covered up by many other strata.

His friends nicknamed him "Strata" Smith and made fun of him for being so interested in layers of rock. But to Smith each stratum, with its shells and other fossils, was a picture of one period of the past, and each stratum could be roughly dated in relation to other strata. Scientists realized the great service he had performed. He had, in fact, helped to lay the foundations of two important sciences: paleontology and geology.

People who were interested in the history of the earth itself soon began to make the sort of diagrams which Smith had made. These diagrams showed how the earth had changed in the past and was still changing. Rock strata that buckled skyward showed that at some time the earth at that place had been heaved upward, sometimes to such a height that a mountain was formed. Each layer of hardened silt showed that at some time the sea had covered that particular place. Some of the diagrams were very complicated, because, as the layers proved, the earth's crust in certain parts of the world had a very complicated history. Over and over again it had heaved upward, worn away, been covered by water and sediment, then heaved upward again.

But even if one cross-section had only six layers in it and another had 106, the diagram makers could match the two together by studying the fossils each layer contained. If the third layer from the top of one diagram contained certain shells, and the thirty-third layer from the top of the other diagram contained the same kind of shells, the scientists knew those two layers had been formed at the same time. When they learned to match layers, the new geologists could begin to solve the mystery of the earth's rocks.

And of course the new cross-section diagrams were very useful to the fossil collectors, too. Now, when they discovered fossil shells or fossil bones, they noted carefully the layer of rock in which each was found. Then they checked those layers on one of the new diagrams, and were able to state which animal had lived first, the one who left the shell behind or the one who left the bone. (Ordinarily, of course, the animal on the lower layer had lived first, as bottom layers were older than top layers.)

When they could do that—when they could put their fossils into some kind of order—they were laying the foundations of the science of paleontology. Then they were able to put all the fossils from one layer together and could begin to understand that certain kinds of animals had lived at one period, and very different kinds of animals had lived at another.

As they made more and more diagrams and learned more and more about the layers of rock beneath the earth's surface, the new geologists saw that the history of the earth could be divided up into several big sections, or eras. During each era there had been, first, a great upheaval which had thrust huge ranges of mountains high into the air. Then, as the mountains wore down from centuries of wind and rain, large parts of the earth's surface had been covered with water and sediment. Afterward, when the waters subsided, there had been more mountain building.

The scientists gave each of the eras a name, made by putting Greek words together. The most recent era—the one that includes our present day and goes back past the last big mountain-building time—they called Cenozoic, which means "of recent life." The one before that they called Mesozoic, or "of in-between life." And the one before that they called Paleozoic, which means "of ancient life."

Below the strata of the Paleozoic era are some which must have been formed even earlier. In these there are comparatively few fossils: rather obscure traces of algae and the trails of wormlike creatures. Scientists have given the name Proterozoic, which means "of earlier life," to this era before the Paleozoic. And to the earliest era of all —so far as rock records show—they have given the name Archeozoic, which means "of beginning life."

But in between the big mountain-building upheavals of each era there had been, the scientists learned, other smaller upheavals. So scientific men divided the big eras up into smaller divisions of time marked off by these smaller disturbances. These divisions are called periods.

Period names were usually invented by the man who first found and diagrammed a complete rock-strata story of the events of that time. And usually the man made up the period name from the location of the rocks he had studied.

The Cambrian period was named by a famous geologist, Adam Sedgwick, who found a clear rock-strata story of that period in the Cambrian Mountains of Wales. The Cambrian is the earliest of the seven periods that make up the big Paleozoic era.

The Jurassic period, which is one of the subdivisions of the Mesozoic era, was named by a man who first diagrammed a complete storytelling sample of the rock strata formed at that time. He did his work in the Jura Mountains of France, and named the period for those mountains. Today wherever similar strata or rock are found—whether it be in Montana or Mongolia—the name Jurassic is used for them, just as the name Cambrian is used for any rocks that were formed contemporaneously with the Cambrian rocks that Adam Sedgwick first diagrammed.

Geologists judge periods chiefly by means of the fossils in the rocks. They work on the general assumption that at any given period life the world over was somewhat similar. So, even though rocks may not look alike, they will still be given the same label if their fossils are those recognized as peculiar to the same period. You may hear a scientist talk of a Cambrian limestone in Brazil, or a Jurassic shale in India. The name does not tell us anything except when that rock was formed.

Periods, in turn, are divided into smaller subdivisions called epochs. The Cenozoic era, for example, consists of two periods which in turn are divided into seven epochs. Working backward from the most recent one—the one that includes our own day—they are named Holocene, (now usually called Recent), Pleistocene, Pliocene, Miocene, Oligocene, Eocene, and Paleocene. All the names come from the Greek language, and each ends with almost the same group of letters that forms the first part of the era's name, Cenozoic. In each case the *ceno* or *cene* means the same thing, "recent." So the names of the various epochs mean "wholly recent," "most recent," "more recent," "less recent," "slightly recent," "dawn of the recent," and "ancient recent." And even if the names do sound a little confusing at first, it's easy to see that they are quite sensible after all.

When the geologists had their diagrams all in order—although of course they are still filling in details to this very day, because the layers of rock in many parts of the earth have not yet been studied—they found they had a kind of outline of the history of the earth.

Their diagrams showed them that the six great continents of our own day, Europe, Asia, North America, South America, Africa, and Australia, had existed as huge masses, at first of rock and later of earth and rock, throughout their entire history. But all the continents had suffered many changes. Sometimes the sea had risen so high that great portions of land were submerged. Sometimes two continents were joined together by a bridge of dry land, as North and South America are today; and sometimes that bridge was submerged and each continent stood separate and alone. Rivers had been born out of streams tumbling down from newly built mountains, and then those rivers had disappeared when the land had worn down to flatness once more. Great masses of ice had covered parts of the continents during periods when the climate was bitterly cold.

But the scientists still didn't know exactly how many millions of years ago the events of the Cambrian period, for example, took place. Even today they are not sure of that. Quite recently, however, they have discovered a new test that is helping them to learn the age of rocks formed in the Cambrian or some other periods.

They worked out this test after they learned that certain elements, such as uranium, are what scientists call unstable. That is to say, uranium does not remain uranium forever. It gradually breaks up, or disintegrates, into other products, and it does this at a known rate that is the same for all uranium.

Uranium breaks up until helium and a specific kind of lead are its end products. Scientists know that the disintegration rate is such that after two billion years one fourth of the uranium has broken down and three fourths is left unchanged.

So, to find the age of uranium-bearing rock, they proceed as follows:

1. They take a piece of mineral that plainly comes from the rock when it was first formed.

2. They determine the proportion of uranium in it to that of the particular kind of lead derived from uranium.

3. Knowing how long it takes for one fourth of the uranium to disintegrate, and knowing the percentage of disintegrated uranium in their piece of rock, they can then figure out how old the rock is.

Of course, relatively few dates can be figured out in this way, and scientists still have many things to learn about the precise datings of various rock strata. They have been able to estimate the approximate time durations of the various eras and periods, however, and by studying fossil animals and their amount of change over the thousands of years, they have some idea of the time at which they may have lived.

Even during William Smith's lifetime—long before the uranium test was invented—scientists had already learned a great deal. They knew something, for instance, of the creatures that lived during the Cambrian and Ordovician periods.

3 five hundred million years ago

FIVE HUNDRED MILLION YEARS AGO, AT THE BEGINNING OF the Cambrian age, the land was a strange and dismal place of naked rock, without a single blade of grass and without a single flower or bush or tree to break the vast expanse of barren stone that stretched from sea to sea. Perhaps in some places at the edge of the water there was a thin greenish film made up of almost invisibly tiny plants called algae, but these patches of slime were the only green things to be seen on shore.

All the life of the whole world, all its color and movement, were in the sea.

The sea was much larger then than it is now. It covered many great low-lying plains that are now dry land. But probably then, as today, most living creatures avoided the deep sea floor, and lived in crowded colonies among the waving water plants that grew close to the shorelines.

Nobody knows exactly how many different kinds of

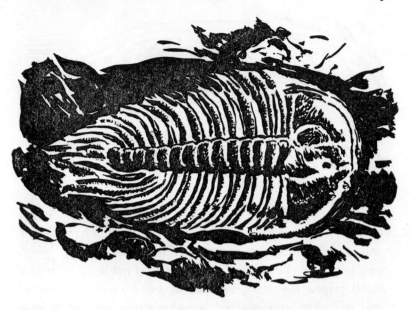

Trilobite fossil

animals inhabited those ancient oceans. Scientists have already identified the fossils of about two thousand different
kinds, or species, but they have no idea how many more
may be discovered in the future. And they cannot even
guess how many other animals living at that time had
such soft bodies that they could leave behind no fossil
clues to their existence.

Of all the fossils found from this period of the earth's
history, the Cambrian period, the greatest number were
left by the group of animals called trilobites. These little
creatures got their name from their appearance. Their
bodies were tri-lobed, or three-lobed. In other words, each
trilobite had a central section, or lobe, running from head

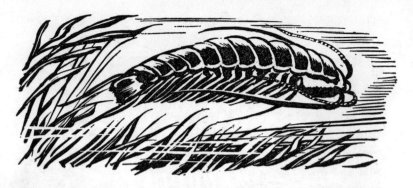

Trilobite

to tail, with a section on either side of it. The trilobite
was divided into three crosswise parts too: head, body,
and tail. The central or body part was made up of many
small joined segments, and could bend easily. The head
and tail were both covered with an armor—really an outside skeleton of a horny substance called chitin, hardened
by calcium carbonate.

A trilobite had many pairs of legs. The lower half of
each leg was stiff and pointed, so that the trilobite could
grip the sea floor when he wanted to crawl ahead or brace
himself against the tug of the current. The legs branched
into two parts and some of the branches carried tiny
featherlike gills, the apparatus through which the trilobite obtained oxygen from the water. Perhaps he could
also use these feathery gills as tiny oars for swimming
along above the sea floor. But some trilobites probably
swam by bending their bodies and then straightening
them out with a quick jerk, much as shrimp swim today.

Most trilobites had eyes, although probably they could
not see well. They also had feelers, like the ones lobsters

have, which waved around as they moved, and helped them to find food or avoid danger.

There were many members of the trilobite family and they varied in their looks and their size. Most of them were less than three inches long, but one rather late member of the group, which lived about 400 million years ago, sometimes grew to a length of two feet. His name, *Isotelus*, means that his head and his tail were nearly alike. *Isotelus* was the giant of the world in his day. No other creature in the seas at that time was as large as he was.

Another class of animals that thrived and grew very numerous during the Cambrian age were the shelled creatures called brachiopods.

A brachiopod had a soft body like a clam's, and lived inside two hinged shells called valves. Inside his shells he sometimes had a stalklike arm which he could thrust out and use for attaching himself to the sea bottom. Some varieties used it for boring holes in the sand, where they could hide.

Brachiopods

Most brachiopods were quite small, ranging from one quarter of an inch to four inches in length. The brachiopods came in an almost endless variety of shapes. Some looked like modern scallops, some like tiny pyramids, some like round cups. Some were smooth. Some had frilled or twisted shells. And their shells might be thin or thick. One variety looked very much like the curved stone bowl that was used as an oil lamp during the days of the ancient Romans. That is why people sometimes use the name "lamp shells" for members of the brachiopod group.

Scientists still do not know how many different kinds of brachiopods there were, but they think there must have been thousands of varieties. At certain places, where billions of their shells became pressed and crushed together, they formed solid beds of what is now limestone. Some

Sponges

Jellyfish

varieties of brachiopods still survive today. They probably look very much like their ancestors of long ago.

There were sponges in the Cambrian seas too, but they were different from most modern members of the sponge family. Their tiny skeletons were made of silica, the same material from which glass is made, so they were hard instead of soft. Little needlelike remains of their skeletons are sometimes found in ancient rocks.

Many kinds of wormlike creatures lived in the water too: round ones, flat ones, thin ones, and fat ones. Their fossil trails and tubes and burrows are found even in rocks older than the Cambrian.

There were jellyfish, also, which probably looked much like modern jellyfish whose slender waving tentacles dangle downward from a soft jellylike body.

Bryozoans

But the snails of five hundred million years ago didn't look much like modern snails. They probably had very flat shells instead of coiled ones. They did crawl slowly about the sea floor, though, just as snails do today, and they burrowed into the mud to hide. In sedimentary rock scientists have found tracks and holes which they think were made by snails living in the Cambrian period.

As millions of years passed, the inhabitants of the sea began to change. Four hundred million years ago the sea was even larger than it had been a hundred million years earlier, and some of the sea animals were increasing in size. The snails, for example, were bigger than they had been, and their shells were beginning to curl.

With the passing of time, some groups of animals had become more prominent. One of these groups was the bryozoans. Their name means "mosslike"; some of these little creatures clung to lamp shells or stones in tightly packed colonies that looked like patches of moss. Other bryozoans formed curious twisted or dome-shaped colonies, or clung together to make a formation that looked like the trunk and branches of a bare tree.

Each tiny bryozoan lived inside a hard tube formed out of the lime in sea water. The only part of the animal that reached outside of this protective tube was a mass of arm-like tentacles, each covered with invisible hairs. As the hairs moved back and forth in the current, they forced small streams of water into the tube. And as the water passed through its body the bryozoan strained out the microscopic plants and animals that were its food. Billions of tiny bryozoan tubes, packed tightly together, have formed beds of limestone.

Another newcomer dating from the Ordovician period was the little animal called a coral, which also took calcium out of the water and built itself a hard limy skeleton. Many of these skeletons, attached to one another, formed all sorts of strange shapes. Near the coast of Australia the Great Barrier Reef, a great wall of coral reaching from the sea bottom almost to the surface of the water, has been built up by countless billions of generations of these tiny creatures. It is five hundred feet high and over a thousand miles long.

Scientists feel sure there were clams in the sea even earlier than four hundred million years ago, but probably the clams that lived before that time did not have hard shells and so could not leave fossils behind. When the clams did begin to have shells they probably looked somewhat like the clams of today, with two shells hinged tightly together.

The clam's most dangerous enemy in those ancient seas was the starfish—an animal that exists today and still eats clams just as his ancestors did. Starfish belong to a family of animals called echinoderms, which means "spiny-skinned." Anyone who has ever felt the rough bumps on the upper surface of a starfish can understand why this name was given to the family.

The undersurface of this creature's starshaped body is equipped with many tiny tubes, which are the animal's feet. But there are also sucking devices at the end of the tubes, and the ancient starfish—like his present-day descendant—used these when he grew hungry enough to attack a clam. He folded his body around a clamshell, attached his tube feet to each half, and tried to pull the hinged shells open. The clam was strong, but the starfish was usually stronger. Finally the two halves of the clamshell separated, and the soft body inside was exposed.

The starfish had no teeth and no tongue, so he could not bite into the clam or lick off a piece to swallow. Instead he thrust his stomach inside out through the hole that was his mouth, pushed his stomach inside the open clamshells, and enveloped the clam's whole body while diges-

Clams and starfish

Crinoids

tive fluids were secreted. When the clam's body was digested, the starfish pulled its stomach back inside its own body and moved off, leaving a pair of empty clamshells behind. When empty shells are found on the sea floor today they often mean what they meant four hundred million years ago: a starfish had a hearty meal.

Another spiny-skinned echinoderm that appeared in the sea at about the same time the starfish did was the crinoid. This creature looked no more like an animal than a starfish did. In fact he looked so much like a flower that he is usually called a sea lily. His head was at the top of a tall stem, or stalk, and he had waving frondlike arms. These sent currents of water into his mouth, so that he could filter out the tiny plants and animals that were his food. But the crinoid was not as delicate as he looked. His entire body was covered with a hard armor plating made of lime.

There are crinoids in the sea today too, and their bodies are still covered with this stonelike armor.

The trilobites remained extremely numerous for about a hundred million years. And by the Ordovician period, when the bryozoans, corals, clams, starfish, and crinoids had made their appearance, another group of animals had become prominent: the cephalopods.

The nautiloids were one type of cephalopod. The very earliest members of this family probably did not have protective shells. By Ordovician times, however, they were living inside cone-shaped homes where they were safe from the attack of other sea creatures.

These cones were built up gradually, as the nautiloids themselves grew. A very young nautiloid lived inside a very small shell, pointed at one end and flaring open at the other. Then, as the nautiloid grew larger and became cramped in such tiny quarters, he built a new and larger

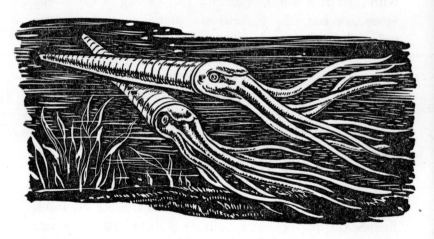

Nautiloids

Sea scorpion

section for living, and walled off the old one with a shell partition. Time after time he repeated this process, building a larger room each time and walling off the old one, until his shell resembled a large, sectioned ice-cream cone with a point at one end and a wide opening at the front, where the nautiloid lived. Some nautiloids gradually developed shells that were curled, like snail shells or like the horns of a buffalo.

Inside the shell the nautiloid's body was soft. Cephalopod, the name of the family to which the nautiloid belonged, means "head-footed." In these animals the foot surrounds the head in a number of tentacles. The nautiloid used its whole body when it wanted to move. It took in water, then squirted the water out quickly through a hole beneath its head, thus creating a water jet that propelled the whole shell backward. This jet-propulsion method of movement is still used today by the squid, which is a distant relative of the nautiloid.

Some nautiloids had beaks and long powerful tentacles. When the nautiloids grew to the amazing length of fifteen feet, as some of them did, they must have been the most terrifying creatures the sea's population had yet known.

But even these powerful cephalopods, after some fifty million years, acquired a worthy competitor in the giant sea scorpion. This animal probably never grew as large as the largest nautiloid. Some sea scorpions were only a few inches long, and the biggest was about ten feet in length. Some had the legs and pointed tail of the present-day land scorpion. Others—the largest ones—were remarkably well equipped for defense and attack. Their bodies were armored with a tough crusty shell and their flattened tails were furnished with spikes. At the end of their thin arms were sharp-toothed pincered claws, like the claws of a lobster, that could catch and hold prey.

Like the nautiloid and the trilobite, the giant sea scorpion belonged to the large group of animals which have no vertebrae, or backbones—the animals called invertebrates. Invertebrates are still extremely numerous in the world to this day, even though certain members of the group—the trilobites, for example—disappeared entirely many millions of years ago.

But by 350 million years ago, part way through the Devonian period, the invertebrates were no longer the only abundant forms of animal life on the earth. The second large group of animals—animals which do have backbones—had become numerous. These are called vertebrates.

ERAS	PERIODS	EPOCHS	DURATION IN YEARS	TOTAL TIME	DOMINANT LIFE
Cenozoic	Quaternary	Recent	10,000	75 Million	man
		Pleistocene	1,000,000		
	Tertiary	Pliocene	8,000,000		mammals
		Miocene	20,000,000		
		Oligocene	10,000,000		
		Eocene	21,000,000		
		Paleocene	15,000,000		
Mesozoic	Cretaceous		65,000,000	135 Million	reptiles
	Jurassic		35,000,000		
	Triassic		35,000,000		
Paleozoic	Permian		25,000,000	300 Million	amphibians
	Pennsylvanian		25,000,000		
	Mississippian		25,000,000		
	Devonian		45,000,000		fishes
	Silurian		35,000,000		
	Ordovician		65,000,000		invertebrates
	Cambrian		80,000,000		
Proterozoic	Upper Precambrian		750,000,000	750 Million	primitive multicellular forms
Archeozoic	Lower Precambrian		750,000,000	750 Million	unicellular forms

4 *the age of fishes*

EVEN BEFORE THE DEVONIAN PERIOD—IN THE SILURIAN period—there was a new group of animals. While some of them fed on the bottom and probably crawled there, they swam, too, somewhat like present-day fish, and their home was in fresh-water lakes and streams.

These new swimmers did not appear suddenly. They had begun to develop far back in the Ordovician period. In the beginning they could hardly swim at all. They could only wriggle along, close to the bottom of the streams and lakes.

In the Silurian period they had not yet developed real vertebrae—the bony segmented rods which most modern fish have inside their bodies. Instead of a backbone they had an elastic cord of cells—a kind of inner axis called a notochord. And these primitive fish did not have jaws. They had to get their food by sucking in water through their jawless mouths and straining out the edible bits of plant and animal matter found in it.

The ostracoderms were one of the first groups of very early fish. Their name means "shell-skinned." Hard bony plates formed an armor over their heads. A flexible armor of smaller plates, neatly fitted together, covered the rest of their bodies.

Two orders of the ostracoderms—the Heterostraci and the Cephalaspida—had very heavy armor, a somewhat flattened shape, and a mouth on the underside of the body. All this evidence suggests that they were sluggish, mud-grubbing creatures that kept close to the bottom of the lakes and streams.

Anaspida

But the Anaspida, the third order of ostracoderms, had lighter armor and appear to have been more active. Although they had no jaws, their mouths were shaped more like those of modern fishes and were on the forward part of their bodies instead of underneath. From this evidence it appears likely that they were beginning to forsake the bottoms of the streams and lakes and to swim about more freely, seeking their food.

By the end of the Devonian period the ostracoderms

had died out. By this time other creatures had appeared which were halfway to becoming modern fish. They still did not have vertebrae made of bone, but they were progressing toward real bony jaws. One such animal was the tiny acanthodian, only a few inches long and covered with an armor of small diamond-shaped scales made of bonelike material. The acanthodian belonged to a big group of bony-jawed fish called Placodermi, or placoderms (plate-skinned fishes).

The placoderms all had some features in common: jaw-like parts of one kind or another; and paired, finlike structures arranged in various ways. These structures gave the placoderms an advantage over the more primitive ostracoderms, as fins are necessary balancing devices for fish that swim.

The placoderms called arthrodires were more prominent than were the acanthodians. They were of varying sizes, some very small, some over thirty feet long. Generally their bodies were shaped somewhat like those of modern fish, with very few bonelike scales. The front half of the trunk was still covered with armor, however, with the head and chest portions separately built but hitched together by elaborate joints. On both upper and lower jaws was a combination of toothlike projections and a shearing edge which may have served as primitive teeth.

By the latter part of the Devonian period, thirty-foot *Dinichthys*, "terrible fish," one of the best known of the arthrodires, was living in salt water. *Titanichthys*, "giant fish," was even larger than *Dinichthys*—possibly forty feet —and could stretch his huge jaws to an opening four feet across. In their day these huge arthrodires must have

Shark

dominated the waters in which they lived, yet they died out at the end of the Devonian period.

One of the most important families of the Devonian period is one that is also most interesting to us today, because its descendants still swarm through our oceans. This is the shark family. Some members were small and some were large, but none had a hard outer armor. Their skin was very tough, and so rough that it felt like sandpaper. Sharkskin is sometimes used as a kind of sandpaper today, in fact, for the polishing of wood and ivory. This tough skin was completely flexible, so that the sharks could twist and dart and swim through the water with great speed. Because they had well-developed jaws, and paired fins arranged on a somewhat "modern" plan, they looked like the sharks of today. Once they appeared on the scene the oceans probably began to resemble our oceans. By this time the upper levels of the water, as well as the bottom of the sea, were becoming inhabited. In fact, the Devonian has been called the Age of Fishes.

The vertebrae, as well as the remainder of the skeleton of the sharks, were made of cartilage, or "gristle," and not of real bone. Today there are dozens of varieties of sharks, and they still have that same kind of cartilagenous skeleton. Modern sharks include some of the biggest and fiercest creatures of the sea. One modern member of the family has acquired great flat wing-shaped pectoral fins on either side of its body, just behind its head, and a tail that has narrowed to a thread. This kite-shaped creature is the modern skate. The manta, or devilfish, which sometimes has a "wing spread" of twenty feet, is also a present-day relative of ancient sharks. So is the giant 45-foot whale shark.

But scientists tell us that another shark about as large as the whale shark did exist for a time about thirty million years ago. They call him *Carcharodon megalodon,* and he was probably a relative of the man-eating shark. The only fossils of this big ancient fish ever found are enormous teeth, some more than four inches long. Jaws big enough to accommodate such teeth would look like the entrance to a cave—a vast gape six feet wide. So, although scientists can't be sure what this giant looked like, they think it must have been nearly forty feet long.

Another group that appeared in the Middle Devonian period have been called the Higher Bony Fishes. They had a kind of outer armor, but it was in fact composed of scales that made them look like modern fish. These ganoid scales, as they are called, were tough and bony on the underside and shiny on top. Their shiny surface gave them their name; ganoid means "glistening."

Among the few members of this "glistening-scaled" family that survive today are the sturgeon, the fresh-water gar pike found in North American waters, and the Mississippi River paddlefish, which is about four feet long and has a long flat snout that looks rather like a canoe paddle.

Teleosts

The skeletons of the Higher Bony Fishes were predominantly bony and only partly made of cartilage. Some of these fish were large and some were small. Some had big jaws and big pointed teeth for snatching at their prey. Others had many smaller teeth, and could probably grind up shelled animals for food.

The Higher Bony Fishes can be divided into two groups: the ray-finned fishes (with fins supported by a skeleton of parallel rays) and the lobe-finned fishes (with fins supported by a single stout "lobe"). In the Jurassic period a group of ray-finned fishes called teleosts appeared. The word teleost means "completely bony," and tells us that these creatures had skeletons made entirely of bone. They had deeply overlapping scales without the glistening ganoid surface, and they had jaws.

One of the early teleosts was the herring, and another was a big fish rather like a modern tarpon. A third was the Giant Bulldog Fish, over fifteen feet long and with powerful jaws that earned him his name.

The teleosts soon outstripped the other more primitive Higher Bony Fishes, and continued to grow more and more important as the centuries rolled by, until today they

Lobefin

dominate the seas. Most of our modern food fish and game fish belong to the teleosts—from the silvery little shiner to the great blue marlin, the swordfish, the mighty sailfish, and the giant 2,000-pound sunfish.

The other group of Higher Bony Fishes, the lobe-fins, were chiefly important in the Devonian period. This group, which also included the lung fishes, lived at first in fresh-water streams and rivers.

A lungfish could breathe even when its head was out of the water, because it had a breathing apparatus very much like a real lung—something no other creature of that time possessed.

The lobe-finned fish could also breathe with its head out of water. It took oxygen from the air by means of its lunglike air bladder, the small air-filled sac inside its body which helped it to balance in the water. It had a long body, a big mouth, a somewhat flattened skull, and two pairs of rounded or lobe-shaped fins. It didn't look very unusual but, as we shall see in Chapter 6, it is very important for a special reason: the descendants of this fish became the first vertebrate land dwellers.

Off the coast of South Africa in 1938 a coelacanth, a member of the lobe-fin group which scientists thought had completely disappeared more than seventy-five million years ago, turned up unexpectedly in a fisherman's net. The men who caught it did not know what it was; they had never seen anything like it. But they were curious, and took it to the local museum. The curator of the museum, Miss Courtenay-Latimer, did not know what it was either, but she sent word about the strange find to an expert named Professor J. L. B. Smith. Then, in order to preserve the fish until the professor arrived, she had it skinned and mounted.

Professor Smith was astonished when he saw the fish and recognized it as a coelacanth. But he was also very upset because there was nothing left of it for him to study except part of its skeleton and the skin. So he decided to

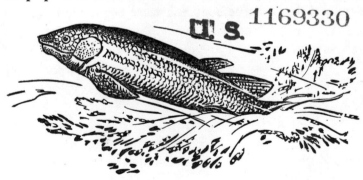

Lungfish

see if a second specimen of this ancient fish could be found. He prepared hundreds of pamphlets describing the coelacanth, and offering a reward for the capture of one. And for many years he traveled up and down the African coast, handing out his pamphlets and urging fishermen to watch for the strange fish described in them.

Fourteen years went by and no coelacanth turned up. Then one day Professor Smith received a radio message telling him that a fisherman of the Comoro Islands, off the coast of Madagascar, was claiming the reward. He set off for Madagascar immediately by plane. And a few hours later he was staring at a new specimen of the fish he had sought so long. It was an important moment in the professor's life and an important moment for all paleontologists. That five-foot-long coelacanth was one of the most exciting clues to the past that had ever come into the hands of the scientific detectives.

Since then still other specimens of this ancient fish have been caught, and scientists are learning more every day about the long-ago time when these creatures were abundant and the first true bony fish were beginning to appear.

5 *the process called evolution*

ABOUT 150 YEARS AGO, WHEN PEOPLE HAD COLLECTED A great many fossils and arranged them in groups according to the rock strata where they had been found, the scientific detectives of that day had solved part of the mystery of the earth's past. From each group of fossils they could deduce the events of one chapter in the history of living things. The fossils had told them, for example, about the backboneless trilobites, once so abundant, and about the fishlike vertebrates that later appeared in the sea. And the fossils told them that at still later periods of history other creatures appeared—dinosaurs at one time and mammals at another.

But the scientists still had no answers to questions like this: Why had the trilobites vanished? Where had the vertebrates come from? What was the explanation of the dinosaurs' amazing appearance at a later time—and of the appearance of the most recent animal, man himself? As long as these questions remained unanswered, part of the story of the earth would remain a mystery.

One scientist, Cuvier, suggested that the answers could be found in the great floods and upheavals recorded by the rock strata of the earth. He said that each of these events had destroyed every creature alive in the world at that time. And after each of those catastrophes, he believed, a new kind of life had been created. After the catastrophe that destroyed the trilobites, for example, the vertebrates had come into being. Then the early vertebrates had been destroyed and still another form of life had appeared. Man himself, the scientist said, had been created after the last of all the earth's many catastrophes.

But not everybody agreed with this suggestion. Many people thought it didn't explain everything. They pointed out that certain creatures, the very early sharks, for example, had continued to exist through many different periods, and still existed in the seas of the modern world. Some better explanation was needed, these people thought, to account for the animals that survived, as well as for the ones that vanished.

Then a better explanation did come along, one that most scientists finally accepted. No single man worked it out. It resulted from the work of many men. They studied fossils and they studied living animals of their own day, and they worked out what they called the theory of evolution.

The word evolution comes from the word evolve, which means "to become developed." And the theory of evolution declares that the very first forms of life on the earth—the jellylike blobs which existed long before the first trilobite appeared—evolved or developed into all later forms of life.

Scientists know that not all those first jellylike blobs turned into trilobites. Today the sea still swarms with tiny invisible bits of life called protozoa, a name that means "first animal." Some modern protozoa are probably like the first and simplest forms of life on the earth. But some of the ancient protozoa, scientists believe, did evolve into trilobites and other creatures of the early Cambrian period. And some of the Cambrian creatures—although the trilobites themselves disappeared—gradually evolved, over many millions of years, into fishlike creatures. And some of these in turn finally evolved still further into the many complicated forms of vertebrate life known on the earth today.

One proof scientists offer for this theory is the fact that they can trace quite clearly some of the steps in the long process of evolution. They can see, for example, how the early jawless, backboneless dwellers of the sea bottom could gradually have developed into true fish with backbones and jaws.

But even the theory of evolution didn't solve the whole mystery. The scientific detectives still didn't know *how* or *why* one kind of creature had evolved into another kind. Had the change taken place by accident? Or on purpose? Had one animal "decided" to evolve into a different kind of animal?

For many years it seemed that this part of the mystery would never be solved. Some parts of it, in fact, have not been solved yet. But about a hundred years ago a very careful and painstaking scientist named Charles Darwin worked out a new theory that explained a good deal about how and why the process of evolution took place.

Charles Darwin was the son of a well-to-do English doctor, and the grandson of a famous scientist. When he was a boy everybody thought he would have a brilliant career, probably in the field of medicine where his father had been so successful. But for a long time Charles disappointed his family, just as young William Smith had disappointed his uncle some half a century earlier. Charles was not interested in studying medicine after his graduation from college. The only things that did interest him were collecting fossils and going hunting. And he spent so much time on these two hobbies that, like young "Strata" Smith, he earned the reputation of being unambitious.

Then one day in 1831, when Charles was twenty-two years old, he was invited to take a five-year trip around the world on the sailing ship, *H.M.S. Beagle*. The *Beagle* was a British Royal Navy vessel, bound on an official voyage to British colonies and other ports. Officials of the Navy had decided that it would be a good idea to take along a young scientist to study the plants and animals in various parts of the world and bring back specimens of those unknown in England. Charles was recommended for the job by one of his college professors who knew that the young man liked to collect fossils.

Today all scientists know the story of *H.M.S. Beagle's* voyage. It is famous because it was during this voyage that Charles Darwin began the long years of work that finally led him to part of the solution so many men had sought. Darwin's contribution to the solution of the mystery was this: the process of evolution is based on *adaptation*, and adaptation occurs through *natural selection*.

He observed that no two plants or animals of a kind are ever born exactly alike. There are always slight differences, or variations, between them. He also observed that in wild life a certain proportion of animals never survive, while others flourish. Darwin's thought was that among plants and animals there is a constant struggle going on— a fight to go on living. It has been called the "struggle for existence." He argued that the slight differences among animals determine which shall survive and which shall die. The successful animals are those with variations which best suit them to living in their particular surroundings. They flourish and have young. Among the young, again, those survive that have favorable variations or that inherit the good characteristics of their parents. In the struggle for existence, thought Darwin, there is a constant weeding out of the weak and unfit and a survival of the fit. This is "natural selection."

But suppose that in time an animal's surroundings change drastically. Suddenly it could happen that the animal is no longer fitted to his environment. Instead, an animal with hitherto unfavorable characteristics might now be the one who was best adapted to survive. The previously favored animal might die out entirely.

Or suppose a few animals of a group migrated to new surroundings. Suddenly a variation that was unfavorable in their old environment might make them well adapted to the new conditions of living. They would have young and some of those too might be well adapted to the new surroundings. They would survive and gradually the group of that particular kind of animal would increase. As animals gradually changed and gradually adapted to new environments, Darwin reasoned, new kinds of animals would develop and older ones would die out.

Darwin thought of natural selection as chiefly brought about by the "survival of the fittest" in the "struggle for existence." Scientists today still recognize the importance of natural selection in evolution, but they have enlarged upon Darwin's theories. Since his time they have learned much about heredity. They now know that in general the young inherit the characteristics of their parents, with, of course, the slight variations which Darwin recognized. These variations make a constant slight difference in animals of a group, and the differences can accumulate by heredity and result over thousands of years in a new type of animal. This is one kind of natural selection.

But besides the small variations, scientists now know that occasionally, for reasons not entirely clear, an animal is born with some feature strikingly different from that of any of its ancestors. This very striking difference, which seems to take the animal off on a new tack, is called a *mutation*. Often a mutation can be so harmful that the animal will not survive. But occasionally a mutation is favorable, and the animal not only survives but has young which inherit the new characteristic. Mutation and its inheritance is another of the ways in which new types of animals evolve.

Scientists today recognize that on an earth as varied as ours there is a vast amount of room for living organisms, and there are an endless variety of conditions for living. Some creatures, just as they are, are perfectly adapted to their environment, and have never changed or been replaced by other forms.

But, over millions of years, most groups of animals have changed. In each generation the changes have been small, but over the thousands of years they have been inherited until their accumulated sum has resulted in new forms of animals. When this has happened, there has not always been a question of struggle and survival—the new forms have not always replaced the older types in their environment. Instead, they have constantly pushed out to whatever new and slightly different spots there is an opportunity to occupy. There they have had a tendency to split up further into varied types of populations. Each of these in turn has settled in some particular spot in the new location and has become more and more specialized and adapted to the particular way of life that location requires. So there has been a tremendous total increase in the areas of the earth that are occupied and in the varieties of animals that occupy them. Animals seem to seize opportunities for living in every possible environment, and they meet these opportunities with the natural equipment they have acquired, often through mutations.

Animals have sometimes seemed to change more or less at random and to spread out haphazardly; yet, scientists say, something must control this spreading and changing. There must be some limit to the changes any animal can make. That is correct; there is a limit. An animal can change along certain lines only, *depending on what he is already*. For instance, a bird might acquire slight changes in its wing structure, but a cat could not suddenly inherit wings.

And an animal can change *only to the extent that he can still survive in some environment open to him*. Unless a change is useful to an animal—or at least nonharmful —he will not survive. The necessity to adapt to surroundings is one of the most important factors controlling evolution.

And when an animal can no longer fit into some possible, available environment, he dies out, or becomes extinct. He may become extinct by gradually changing so much that he is no longer the same animal he was before; or he may be completely replaced by another group of animals better fitted to live in his environment; or he may simply die and no other animal take his place.

Evolution seems to have no fixed plan, but this much seems clear. In the development of animals something is always happening. What happens may open up an opportunity for a new way of life to an animal. Animals meet their opportunities with the equipment that is available to them. If their equipment is suitable, they are successful and in time may move into even narrower environments, where they may change into more specialized forms. If their equipment is unsuitable, they will probably become extinct. Evolution comes about through a constant interplay between living organisms and their environments.

6 *the great landward migration*

THE GREAT LANDWARD MOVEMENT OF SEA PLANTS AND SEA animals began about 325 million years ago, and changed the world forever after.

Before that time the whole face of the land had remained barren and empty. While seas, lakes, and rivers teemed with creatures that crawled and swam, the shores around them lay grim and dark. Not a single sprouting plant pushed up through the rock that was slowly crumbling into soil. Not a moving creature stirred on the continents' flat plains and rugged hillsides. No bird or insect flew through the air above.

And then at last the great landward migration took place, and the whole earth became transformed.

Plants were the first living things to establish themselves on the unexplored area of the dry land. They did not actually move onto the land. The migration began when a period of drought occurred—when lakes and rivers began to dry up, and the seas shrank. As the water level dropped all over the world, some plants were partly exposed to the unfamiliar air. And then one day—along the shore of an inland lake perhaps—certain plants were left completely exposed. Some of them withered and died almost immediately. Others were still alive when a shower fell and the water rose again; they were temporarily revived.

But the lake went on shrinking. After a while those plants close along the shores were under water less and less often. And at last there came a day when the water had receded so far that it never touched them again.

A great many of the plants died then, no doubt. But some, which had already been evolving into new types during the lake's slow shrinking period, were somehow able to survive in this new environment.

Afterward they went on changing and developing, and spreading farther and farther inland. At the end of about fifty million years—and scientists say this is a very short time for such an accomplishment—plants covered huge areas of the once barren earth.

Those first land plants did not look much like the trees and bushes of today. None had flowers, and none had the kinds of leaves found on modern plants. But some did look a little like a modern fern with long stalks and tiny fronds, and some were rather like the modern plants called horsetails. Others still looked like green seaweed, however, with ribbonlike arms that lay almost flat on the ground. And still others looked like fat tree trunks that ended in spiky tufts instead of spreading branches.

These curious plants were the ancestors of all the flowers and bushes and grasses and trees that came after them.

They were the beginning of all the green growing things of the earth—the rich carpet of vegetation that makes the earth beautiful, and that directly or indirectly furnishes food for land animals and for mankind.

The first animals that ventured out onto land were the very ones we might expect. They were distant relatives of the trilobites and the sea scorpions, which had already proved that members of their big and numerous family could survive all sorts of conditions and develop in many directions. The scientific name of that family is arthropod, which means "having jointed legs," and the particular joint-legged arthropod that first explored the land probably belonged to the sea-scorpion branch. Not long afterward other members of the arthropod family came ashore too—spiderlike creatures of several varieties, and insectlike creatures that developed into land-dwelling cockroaches.

Perhaps the first land explorers skittered out of the water only occasionally, and in that way acquired, after many generations, the ability to live in the dry air. Some of them must have leaped from plant to plant until, after thousands of generations, they evolved into creatures that could really fly. The cockroaches, for example, developed hard shell-like wings. Other creatures acquired wings that were delicate and transparent. One of the inhabitants of the world's first green forests was a huge dragonfly with wings that measured more than two feet from tip to tip. That particular kind of dragonfly was the largest insect that has ever existed. It died out many millions of years ago.

All the insects of our own day—such as flies, bees, ants,

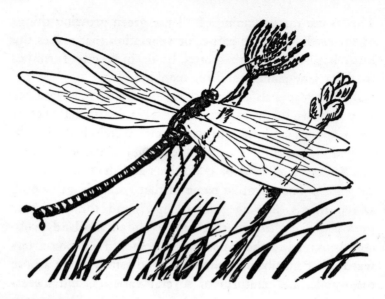

Dragonfly

beetles, lice, and butterflies—have evolved from the first
land dwellers of the arthropod family. Some modern insects, however—the mosquitoes, for example—still return
to the water at least once during their lifetime. Mosquitoes always lay their eggs in a quiet pool or some other
moist place, and those eggs hatch into tiny wormlike
larvae which live in the water until they change into tiny
creatures able to fly. Every cluster of mosquito eggs, float-
ing like scum on the surface of a pond, is a reminder that
once all insects spent their whole lives in the water—
that insects, like all other forms of life, came originally
from the sea.

Somehow it is not too difficult to imagine sea scorpions
scuttling up onto a beach for the first time. This is prob-

ably because tiny crabs and other similar creatures still come out of the water today and scurry around for a while, looking quite at home, before they return to the water. It is harder to imagine fish coming out to live on the land. Yet that is just what the descendants of the remarkable lobe-finned fish did, about three hundred million years ago, toward the end of the Devonian period. Those ancient relatives of the still existing coelacanth became the ancestors of all land-dwelling backboned animals on the earth today. They were the ancestors of frogs, snakes, and birds; of four-footed creatures like cows, dogs, and horses; and of that two-footed animal, man himself.

Of course the lobe-finned fish did not "decide" to move out onto the land, any more than the first land plants deliberately left their home in the water. The fish found themselves on land for the same reason the plants did: the water in which they lived—the inland seas and rivers —suddenly began to shrink during the time of severe drought.

The rivers shrank from broad bands of swiftly running water to slender trickles and a few shallow pools separated from each other by wide stretches of mud or stones. Then the last trickles dried up too. Nothing was left but the shallow pools, and even they were rapidly disappearing.

In each of those pools were several fish—the only fish still alive out of all the sleek creatures that had once swum in those life-giving waters. The fish that stayed in the bed of each stream as it grew narrower and narrower had already perished. And now the fish in the pools were beginning to gasp weakly and die too, as their small crowded homes grew smaller and more crowded each day.

Two kinds of fish managed to survive this catastrophe, however—the slender lungfish and the medium-sized, heavily-scaled lobe-fin.

The lungfish—creatures which, unlike all other fish, had lungs as well as gills—burrowed down into the moist earth, leaving a small air hole that supplied them with all the oxygen they needed. Curled up tightly, with their tails over their heads, they went into a kind of deep sleep. They kept alive by consuming the fat stored up in their bodies, just as modern bears stay alive in a dormant condition during their long period of winter rest. If the drought lasted too long, so that the fat was all consumed, the lungfish starved to death. But if the drought came to an end and they could emerge into the water before their food reserve was gone, they remained alive.

Lungfish still exist today in certain parts of South America, Australia, and Africa. When the fresh-water streams they inhabit dry up each summer, the African and South American varieties still burrow down into the earth and stay alive until the rains come again. Probably they can survive even if there is no rain at all during certain years. At any rate, a group of scientists in New York did keep one lungfish alive in a lump of hardened mud for more than four years.

Three hundred million years ago the second kind of fish, the lobe-finned fish, did not try to burrow into the ground when the pools dried up. These fish, too, could obtain oxygen from the air, but if they remained very long out of water they died. So, when their pools had completely disappeared, some of them used their sturdy lobe-shaped fins to push themselves along over the mud in search of a hollow that still held a little water.

Some of them managed to reach other pools not too far away and plopped into them just in time. They had saved their lives. And in their fight for survival they had been land dwellers for at least a short time. They had made evolutionary history.

Probably that single journey did not bring an end to the lobe-fins' troubles. The pools they had reached with such difficulty would not have sheltered them for long. Those pools too would soon have dried up, and when the water disappeared, again only some of the gasping lobe-fins would have been able to reach another pool quickly enough to save themselves.

As more and more pools dried up, some of the fish must have had to attempt land travel over and over again. Those that continued to survive until the rains fell and the rivers filled up were those with the strongest fins and with air bladders best equipped for taking oxygen from the air over long intervals.

Many of the young of those surviving fish inherited their parents' strong fins and good air bladders, and during each dry season they too were able to move across the ground to seek the water they needed. After many generations their bladders were more and more like real lungs, and they could remain out of the water for a longer period than could their ancestors. Their fins had become steadily stronger and had also changed shape. The bony skeleton of those fins had come to look very much like a shortened version of the skeleton of a leg and foot. Those fins had evolved, in other words, into primitive legs and feet. And the lobe-fin itself had evolved into what scientists call an amphibian. The word means "leading a double life," and the first amphibian earned his name by living part of the time in the water and part of the time on land. He was the first land-dwelling vertebrate and the ancestor of all land-dwelling animals.

With each passing century more and more of the earth was covered with growing plants. The climate became gentle and damp over huge areas. Low plains were transformed into swamps cut by sluggish streams and set with low islands.

For the newly developed amphibians these conditions were very satisfactory indeed. Slowly, on their short stubby legs, they could move from stream to swampy shore to dry hillock and back again. The land, now carpeted with green and alive with insects, supplied them with as much food as they could find in the water.

As the centuries passed, the first amphibians evolved in many ways. Their bodies were no longer covered with a heavy armor of scales. Instead, they acquired a tough skin that was better suited for life on land. But in general they remained heavy, fat, slow-moving animals.

They were awkward because their bodies were still very much like the bodies of their fish ancestors. The heavy bones and flesh of those ancestors had been supported by the water, but amphibians, when they were on land, had to support their own bodies. And while fish propelled themselves forward by moving their bodies and tails from side to side and using their fins only to balance themselves

Diplocaulus

in the water, the amphibians' tails were of no use in moving over the ground. In order to move at all, amphibians had to carry themselves on their newly acquired legs, and those legs were not yet very well adapted to this difficult task. So they all crept along close to the earth, and had to make a great effort to crawl over even the slightest obstacle.

A curious, rather small creature called *Diplocaulus*, for example, spent almost no time at all on land. He had tried it for a time, but then had gone back to living on the bottoms of muddy streams. His head was enormous, with winglike extensions at each side so that it looked like a broad arrowhead. And his legs were so weak that they could not very well lift his great heavy-headed body off the ground. That is why *Diplocaulus* returned to the water. He even breathed with gills, as his fish ancestors

Eryops

had. He was an "unsuccessful" amphibian. He had given up the struggle to lead a real double life.

A group of amphibians called Rhachitomi proved much better adapted to life on land. Their backbones were strong and stiff and their legs were quite powerful, so that it was fairly easy for them to keep their bodies from sagging onto the ground.

One of the larger amphibians among the Rhachitomi was a creature which scientists call *Eryops;* he sometimes grew to a length of nine feet. His fossil remains are those of a powerful, short-limbed animal. He could not move quickly and could never have escaped from a swift-footed enemy. It was fortunate for him that there were not yet any such animals in the world.

Eryops was born in the water, as were all other amphibians. And the animals had to return to the water to lay

their eggs, because these were enclosed in soft sacs, as
fish eggs are, and would have dried up if they had been
deposited on dry land. The life story of each amphibian
was the life story of the whole amphibian group: it began
in the water and ended with a half-water, half-land existence.

This half-and-half kind of life was not really very efficient. Amphibians got along well enough so long as the
climate stayed warm and damp; and it did stay that way
for what seems to us a very long time, for perhaps fifty
million years. But then the climate changed. While huge
new mountain ranges were being thrust high into the air,
and while the sea fell back away from the new steep
lands, the weather shifted abruptly from hot to cold and
from wet to dry. Great sheets of ice formed over vast
areas of the continents.

Few amphibians were equipped to stand these changes.
Some returned to the water and resumed an aquatic life.
Others—many others—perished. Even the powerful giant
Eryops became extinct. But a few amphibians evolved into
animals able to survive on the new cold earth—animals
that spent their entire life on land.

Today only a few amphibians exist in our modern
world. The salamander is one of them. But the most
familiar modern amphibians are the frogs and the toads.
They seem small and helpless, but they are really better
equipped for life on land than huge *Eryops* was. They do
not have to drag around a heavy tail, because they have
lost their tails entirely. And their back legs are long and
strong, so that they can leap to safety when they are in
danger. But frogs and toads are born legless. Baby frogs,

called tadpoles, look somewhat like tiny fish. And adult frogs must return to the water to lay their eggs. Because of this half-and-half life they cannot compete very well with better-equipped land animals. It is not surprising that frogs and toads are not as important in the world as were their ancestors in the days when amphibians had the land almost to themselves.

The insects of that long-ago period survived the changes of climate better than the amphibians did. In fact, they survived all the changes in the earth's history, and kept evolving and increasing into new varieties. Scientists think there are probably ten million kinds of insects in the world today, although so far they have studied and classified less than one million of them.

The dank forests died away about 250 million years ago, as the weather changed at the end of the Age of Amphibians. Some of the plants evolved into ancestors of our modern trees, but others disappeared entirely. The ancient forests did, however, leave the world a very important legacy. In certain sections, where the ground was wet and marshy, the trees had shot up quickly to great heights, then toppled over into the still pools at their feet. As the centuries passed, those fallen tree trunks formed layers of rotting vegetation that grew thicker year after year. When thick layers of sediment piled up on these layers of rotten vegetation and squeezed them tightly downward, they eventually became coal.

Today we can trace the location of the largest and finest forests of that ancient period by looking at a map of the world's best coal fields. This map tells us that those forests once stood in Pennsylvania—some of the coal beds there are one hundred feet thick—and in England and Russia and many other parts of the world.

The period when coal was being formed used to be called the Carboniferous, from the Latin word *carbo*, which means coal. But because scientists went to Pennsylvania to make studies of the rock strata formed in this period, the second half of the Carboniferous is now usually called the Pennsylvanian period; and the first half is usually called the Mississippian period, because studies of the rock strata formed in those years have been made in the Mississippi Valley.

No other time in the world's long history was exactly like those millions of years when strange forests covered the earth and strange awkward animals moved slowly among them. No other time ever transformed our planet so completely. At its beginning the land had been bare and empty. At its end the land was green with plants and swarming with living creatures. And through all the changes that came afterward, some of those plants and some of those creatures managed to cling fast to the new home they had found after their migration inland from the sea.

7 *early reptiles*

IT WAS DURING THE PERMIAN PERIOD—THE MOST RECENT OF the seven periods of the great Paleozoic era—that the amphibians began to die out because their environment was changing. The climate was no longer warm and damp, as it had been earlier. Great new mountain ranges had been pushed up on the continents and many low water-covered areas had lifted so high that the water drained away from them, leaving their surfaces to bake dry in the open air. A great cold settled over some parts of the earth. Streams and lakes froze solid or dwindled away.

The animals that took over the earth as the great amphibian population died out looked at first very much like their amphibian ancestors. They were very like them, in fact, except for one thing. They had gradually come to possess a single quality which no backboned animal had ever possessed before: they laid eggs which were covered with a firm protective shell lined with a thin membrane. Perhaps the first creature to lay an egg of this kind was an awkward big-headed animal called *Seymouria*. Scien-

Seymouria

tists gave him that name when they first found his fossil
remains near the town of Seymour in northern Texas.

The ability to lay a hard-shelled egg—an egg that had
already been fertilized inside the female's body—may not
seem very remarkable. And perhaps it wasn't a particularly useful accomplishment when it first occurred. So long
as all amphibians had the opportunity to lay and fertilize
their eggs in the water, those eggs needed no more protection than the jellylike membranes which covered them.
Oxygen could get through those membranes to the tiny
embryos inside, and the surrounding water kept the embryos from drying up before they hatched.

Dimetrodon

But as great portions of the earth became less moist, it happened that the animal best suited to survive was the one that could lay a hard-shelled, already fertilized egg. That kind of egg could be laid on the dry ground. A space between its shell and its inner membrane lining served as a sort of lung, providing enough oxygen to keep the embryo alive. The egg also had its own water supply, contained within another membrane. And it had a yolk, a source of food for the tiny life that was coming into being inside the egg.

The creature that emerged from this particular kind of

egg did not have to spend the first part of its life in the water. It had remained inside its protective shell all during its early development, and it hatched out as a true land animal, able to crawl about on its own small legs. It was the first exclusively land vertebrate in the world. Scientists have given it the name reptile, which means "one who creeps or crawls."

Traces of the earliest type of reptiles, called cotylosaurs, are found in the Pennsylvanian period. They were the basic reptiles from which later varieties developed. They appear to have been numerous during the Permian period, then to have died out. *Seymouria* was one of these.

Late in the Pennsylvanian period the basic reptiles started to branch out in varied types. In the beginning all the varieties had the stubby legs of an amphibian, splaying sideward from their bodies when they were not in motion. But in many ways the new animals were changing their looks and their habits.

As early as the Pennsylvanian period one group, called pelycosaurs, had branched from the cotylosaurs. Many of the pelycosaurs looked like their basic reptile ancestors, with sprawling legs, and bodies that were only a little less clumsy than those of the earlier reptiles. But some of the pelycosaurs were becoming more specialized. One creature called *Dimetrodon* and another called *Edaphosaurus*—his long name simply means "ground lizard"—had rows of stiff bony spines standing straight up from their backs. A leathery skin, stretching from spine to spine rather like the webbing between a duck's toes, looked like a huge spread-out fan or sail. Modern scientists do not know what these sails were used for, or if they had any real use at all.

One conjecture is that they served to radiate heat, and so control internal temperature.

Dimetrodon and *Edaphosaurus* looked very much alike, but there was one important difference between them. *Edaphosaurus* had blunt, peglike teeth set in his small head, and he ate nothing but plants. He was what scientists call a herbivore, or plant eater. But *Dimetrodon* belonged to the other great class of animals called carnivores, or meat eaters. The teeth in his large fierce jaws were sharp and pointed, and he was a dangerous enemy to animals smaller and weaker than himself—and perhaps even to big *Edaphosaurus*—because he regarded each one as a possible meal.

In reality both herbivores and carnivores depended on plants. Herbivores ate plants directly, and carnivores ate plant-eating animals. But the difference between the two is still important, because it helps explain why certain animals developed in certain ways.

Meat-eating animals, for example, whether they are large or small, are almost always fierce. If they survive for a long time it is usually because they grow steadily more skillful at attacking and killing other animals. They acquire bigger and sharper teeth, strong claws, tusks, or other weapons. On the other hand, herbivores, which never kill animals for food, usually survive for other reasons. Survival, for them, depends upon the ability to escape or to defend themselves, rather than upon the ability to attack. Sometimes they acquire shells or other kinds of "armor" for protection against the murderous carnivores. Their teeth are not suitable for slaughtering other animals, but only for tearing leaves off trees, chopping up

Edaphosaurus

green stalks and stems, and for pulling up roots and soft water plants.

Throughout the Permian and Triassic periods the reptiles changed little by little. Some remained fairly small—perhaps five or six feet long or less. Some were only as large as a small dog. Many of these small reptiles acquired rather long, strong legs that gave them considerable speed. Other reptiles grew larger and larger. They were evolving toward the group of giant reptiles usually called dinosaurs.

All reptiles—whether small, medium-sized, or large—were either herbivores or carnivores. And the smallest carnivore was fiercer than the largest herbivore. All the herbivores nibbled peacefully at the new shrubs and trees that were beginning to replace the soft swampy growth of the coal-forming periods. The climate of the earth was

Cynognathus

growing steadily warmer again, and they could usually
find plenty to eat. Their chief problem was to avoid their
natural enemies, the carnivores, who continually stalked
the earth in search of prey.

One group of reptiles important during the Permian
and Triassic periods were the therapsids which arose from
pelycosaurs. Some were herbivorous and some carnivorous.
They were immensely varied, but there were three main
divisions: the theriodonts, the dinocephalians, and the dicynodonts.

The theriodonts had heavy tails, like most reptiles, but
their strong legs lifted their bodies up off the ground.
Their heads were shaped rather like dogs' heads; one
member of the family has even been named *Cynognathus*,
which means "dog-jawed." Scientists say these animals
were the ancestors of all mammals, the large group of
creatures that would finally take over the world when the
Age of Reptiles came to an end.

Certain things about *Cynognathus* show very clearly that he was a link between reptiles and mammals. His skull and his skeleton were already becoming more like that of a mammal. And he did not have merely one kind of teeth—biting teeth or grinding teeth. He had both kinds. In the front of his strong jaws were small, sharply pointed teeth for nipping and biting, and at the rear were big flat teeth for chewing or grinding. On either side, between the small teeth and the larger ones, were long teeth like tiny daggers. Human beings and most other mammals have this same general arrangement of teeth; and two teeth on each jaw are still called canines, or dog teeth. The group to which *Cynognathus* belonged, the theriodonts, got their name from the Greek words for "wild beast" and for "teeth." The name indicates that they had teeth like the beasts or mammals.

But these special and interesting qualities of *Cynognathus* probably did not make him seem important at a time when so many bigger animals were beginning to appear.

Big awkward *Moschops*, for example, must have seemed

Moschops

much more outstanding at that particular time. *Moschops* means "young calf face," and the animal's big head did look rather like the head of a young cow. His body reared up on strong legs, and his back sloped downward from his shoulders. He was a rather frightful creature, but his jaws were really weak; he was a plant eater.

Moschops belonged to the suborder of therapsids called dinocephalians, which means "terrible-headed." All were large and powerful and many of them were carnivores, so that in general they were a dangerous group of animals.

The other main group of therapsids, the dicynodonts, were the commonest of reptiles during the Permian period. This large group included big animals and small ones, but they all had one thing in common: their legs did not spread awkwardly sideward. Instead their knees and elbows were brought snugly beneath their bodies. This gave all dicynodonts a better, firmer means of support than other reptiles had. For them, moving about was not a slow and difficult process. They could really stride across the earth in a way no animal before them had done.

The dicynodonts had rather pointed and beaklike skulls and almost no teeth. In fact, in many cases the females appear to have had no teeth at all, while the males had only two tusklike teeth in the upper jaw. "Two dog teeth" is the meaning of their long name.

Big awkward *Moschops* survived for a comparatively short time. By the end of the Permian period, the last period in the Paleozoic era, he was already nearly extinct. The dicynodonts would not last much longer either. And *Cynognathus*, ancestral to the future mammals, would also not survive much longer in his original form.

But during the Permian period there also lived some other creatures which have a special interest for modern scientific detectives.

One was *Eunotosaurus*, which may have been the reptilian ancestor of the turtle. From the Middle Permian period, he did not look much like a modern turtle, but he is interesting because he may have evolved into a creature that survived from very ancient times right up to the present. He probably had a longish neck and a small turtlelike head. But his most important characteristic was his rib formation—eight ribs so wide that their edges almost touched. This arrangement may have been a forerunner of the wide plates which developed later and which form the turtle's shell today.

Other creatures that scientists today find particularly interesting are the rather small Permian reptiles which belonged to the group called Eosuchia, or "dawn crocodiles." They looked rather like lizards, with long bodies and slender legs. There were sharp teeth in their pointed jaws. No one but an expert would be able to realize why these particular little animals were so important. But experts notice that certain openings in their skull bones were like the openings in the skull bones of the great dinosaurs that were soon to develop. The experts think, therefore, that dawn crocodiles belonged to the group of animals that would prove to be ancestors of lizards, flying reptiles, and birds, as well as of the huge reptiles called dinosaurs, best known of all prehistoric animals.

Scientists have not yet searched over the earth in every square foot of land where they believe fossils might be found, but they already know about many areas where certain ancient animals lived.

Fossil beds in Texas, for example, have yielded remains of *Seymouria*, the amphibianlike ancestor of the reptiles, and of many representatives of the early reptiles themselves. Russia, South Africa, western China, and Brazil are some of the other places where many reptile fossils have been found.

The early reptiles were probably spread out pretty well all over the earth. Land bridges then probably connected North America and Asia, North and South America, North America and Europe, Western Asia and Africa, and Asia and Australia. The reptiles could wander from place to place more freely than land animals can today. The climate everywhere was apparently fairly mild. A reptile that could live comfortably in South America could wander up into North America and live just as comfortably there.

It is not very often that the actual flesh of any ancient animal is preserved, even under the most favorable conditions. Bones crumble easily too, or may be crushed among the tumbling stones of a river bed or glacier, unless buried soon after the animal's death. Teeth, however, are likely to last longer than most parts of an animal's body, and paleontologists are glad that reptiles shed their teeth frequently. Because of this trait, scientists have been able to find thousands and thousands of reptile teeth. And with only a handful of teeth to serve as a clue a real expert can sometimes make a very good guess about an ancient reptile.

Of course the teeth alone would not tell the story. But

if an expert has once seen a complete fossil skeleton of a particular kind of animal—and it does quite often happen that a perfect skeleton is found, with every part intact— he can use it as a guide, or standard. Then later, if he finds teeth or other bony parts exactly like those of that skeleton, he deduces that they once belonged to the same kind of animal.

This is one more example of the many kinds of detective work that the paleontologists must do. They have still not solved all the mysteries of prehistoric animals, and of how one group may have evolved from another. They are quite certain, for example, that reptiles like the little Eosuchia evolved into another group of small reptiles shortly after the great Paleozoic era ended and the Mesozoic began. But the mystery of how these second small animals, called thecodonts, eventually evolved into all the many dinosaurs of all sizes and of many strange shapes has not yet been completely solved.

8 *the first dinosaurs*

THE LITTLE THECODONTS, DESCENDANTS OF THE "DAWN crocodile," had to live through a time of change and upheaval. The beginning of each new era in the world's history is always a time of change—of upthrusting mountains and the draining of seas—and the earth-shifting revolution that took place about two hundred million years ago and that marks the division between the Paleozoic and the Mesozoic eras was a particularly powerful one. New mountain ranges were formed. The weather turned cold again. Glaciers covered great areas in the Southern Hemisphere, and green valleys became dry deserts. Hardy plants with scanty foliage that demanded little moisture survived into the new era to become the ancestors of modern pine trees and other evergreens. But many other plants perished.

Many animals also perished at that time. But the primitive turtles managed somehow to survive. So did some of the small creatures that would one day evolve into the

Saltoposuchus

whole great family of mammals. And so did the little thecodonts.

A typical example of the thecodont group was *Saltoposuchus*, a small reptile that lived during the Triassic period. He did not creep slowly along on heavy awkward legs, as the earlier reptiles did. His body, which was only about four feet long, was light and slender and nimble. His legs were slender, too. But though the hind legs were strong and quite long, the front legs were less strong and were very short indeed. In fact, those front legs had become primitive arms, ending in sharp handlike claws, and *Saltoposuchus* did not use them for moving about. Instead he walked only on his hind legs, and used his front claws for grasping things. This made him look very different from all the animals that had come before him.

He did not walk in a completely erect position. That

development was still far in the future. His body slanted upward from the tip of his tail to the top of his head. The weight of his tail actually helped him to balance on his hind legs.

In this slanting, half-erect position, *Saltoposuchus* could move quickly over the ground. He could scurry for safety when he was in danger, and he could chase smaller animals and catch them between his little claws. The footprints he left in the earth looked like the light, pronged footprints of a bird.

His skull was rather large for his body, but the bones of it were light enough so that his head did not sag heavily downward. He had big eyes, strong jaws, and sharp teeth. Because of all these advantages he and similar thecodonts were animals equipped to do many things—animals very well fitted to survive even under difficult and changing conditions.

But their descendants, as they scattered throughout the earth and became adapted to special environments, evolved into many very specialized forms, and lost some of the advantages of their all-round ancestors. Some of them returned to their ancestral home, the water, and some found a new home in the air. Others became so huge that they could no longer move quickly; they could scarcely drag themselves along. Still others developed curious weapons of defense or attack which made them the most fearsome monsters the world has ever seen.

All the large and small land-dwelling descendants of the thecodonts are usually called dinosaurs. This name does not tell us anything about them. No one word could do that, because each descendant was quite different from all the rest. But the word does tell us something about the scientists' struggle to explain the mystery of the past.

Before the science of paleontology came into being about 150 years ago, many people believed that there had once been human giants on the earth. One reason for their belief was that they occasionally found an enormous leg bone or part of a huge skeleton half buried in the ground. They did not know that these were animal bones. They took for granted that they were the bones of enormous men who had lived at some ancient time.

Then certain people who had studied human anatomy declared that those bones had never belonged to human beings. They said they must instead be the bones of very large ancient animals belonging to the reptile group. And an Englishman named Sir Richard Owen, a doctor and also a student of anatomy, invented a name for all those huge creatures—the name dinosauria, which means "terrible lizard." He thought one name would do for the whole group because he believed there had been only a few kinds of these ancient animals, and that they had all closely resembled the lizards of our own day.

But later scientists gradually realized that there had been a great many varieties of ancient reptiles, and that not all of them had been large and terrible. And as they learned more about each separate variety they gave each one a name, often invented with the help of the Greek word *sauros*, which really means "lizard," but which is often translated as "reptile." (True lizards, both ancient and modern, form only one family in the big reptile group.) As soon as the individual names were invented, all scientists began to use them. They had come to realize that it was not accurate to lump all large ancient reptiles together under the one vague and misleading word "dinosaurs."

But in the meantime the whole world had become very excited at the thought that giant animals had once roamed the earth. Newspapers frequently published stories about the finding of what was always called a dinosaur bone, and every amateur fossil hunter dreamed of finding his own dinosaur skeleton. Soon people had talked and read so much about dinosaurs that they felt very familiar and at home with that word.

The word is still widely used today. But it is important to remember that it is not really a scientific word. It refers to a particular group of reptiles, but it does not describe any single one of the many large—and small—creatures which were dominant during the second part of the Age of Reptiles.

Today scientists divide all descendants of the thecodonts into two separate orders, depending on the arrangement and shape of each animal's hipbones. These important bones determine the way an animal walks and holds his body.

One group is called Saurischia, which means "lizard-hipped" or "reptile-hipped." The other is called Ornithischia, which means "bird-hipped."

In the beginning, many members of the Saurischian, or lizard-hipped, group were small, even smaller than *Saltoposuchus*. Tiny *Compsognathus*, for example, was hardly bigger than a good-sized bird. But as the weather grew slowly warmer and milder during the Triassic period—the first of the three periods that make up the Mesozoic era—some of the Saurischians grew larger. At the same time they were evolving in two directions. Some, like *Compsognathus*, continued to walk on two feet like their nimble ancestor *Saltoposuchus*, and to catch animals for food. Others grew so large that they could no longer carry themselves in a half-upright position and had to return to the older method of walking on all four legs. But their front legs usually remained shorter than their hind legs. This gave them a queer, forward-slanting posture, with their hips higher than their shoulders. They could not move quickly enough to catch animal food, so they began to live on plants instead.

During the Triassic period one of the most prominent lizard-hipped dinosaurs was *Plateosaurus*, or "flat lizard," whose fossils have been found in Europe and Asia. He must have seemed a giant in his day, although many dinosaurs were to outgrow him later on. His head was small, but he had a long neck and a long tail, so that he measured about twenty feet in all. He was not so large that he could not stand at least part of the time on his hind legs. But his teeth were rather blunt, which suggests that he may have lived partially on leaves and plants.

By the second period of the Mesozoic era, the Jurassic period which began about 150 million years ago, some of the lizard-hipped dinosaurs were becoming real giants.

The part of North America that is now western Canada and the states of Wyoming, Utah, and Colorado was rich in dinosaur life during the late Jurassic period. The rising seas, flooding southward from the Arctic, had thrust a wide tongue of water across that area. Shallow pools and

Plateosaurus

marshes stretched as far as the eye could see. The air was warm and moist, like that of the tropics. Ferns and palms and water plants grew everywhere, and among them moved the dinosaurs.

One of the largest was the upper Jurassic creature, *Allosaurus*. He had to balance himself with his powerful tail when he stood on his hind legs. From the tip of that tail to the tip of his nose, *Allosaurus* was about thirty-five feet long. The only small things about him were his fore-legs, which were short and almost useless-looking. But there were sharp claws at the ends of them and there were fierce teeth in the jaws of his huge head.

The animal best equipped to escape his clutching claws was a small member of the same lizard-hipped group— graceful little *Ornitholestes*, which was only about five or six feet long. *Ornitholestes* could usually move swiftly enough on his small birdlike feet to avoid his huge and frightening cousin.

But some other of the lizard-hipped dinosaurs were more ponderous. Among the biggest were *Brontosaurus* and *Diplodocus*. These creatures looked terrifying, but they were, in fact, plant eaters without sharp teeth and claws for defending themselves against meat-eating *Allosaurus*. Moreover, they were big and heavy and although they stood on all four legs these could scarcely bear their weight. The best defense of these animals was to keep out of *Allosaurus's* way. They spent most of their time moving slowly and sluggishly through the water, which helped support them and also kept them out of reach of their bloodthirsty enemy.

Brontosaurus means "thunder lizard." Probably the

Ornitholestes

man who invented the name thought this creature was so big that the earth thundered under its feet. *Brontosaurus* was probably about sixty-seven feet long, from the small head on the end of his neck to the point of his long whip-like tail. His legs were enormous, like huge pillars. They needed to be large, for *Brontosaurus* weighed about thirty tons!

Plant-eating, four-footed *Diplodocus* was even longer than *Brontosaurus*. Though his body was not so massive as that of *Brontosaurus*, his long neck thrust far in front of him and a long tail dragged far behind. He was only about sixteen feet tall at the high point of his hips, but from tip of head to tip of tail he sometimes measured 87½ feet. He could swallow only small bits of food at a time because his head was so tiny and his neck was so thin. Scientists think he must have had to keep eating steadily all day long in order to take in enough food to keep his big body alive.

When animals are busy eating they are not likely to notice the approach of an enemy, but *Diplodocus* could protect himself in the same way *Brontosaurus* did. He could stay in a deep pool, stretching down to nibble at the water plants on the bottom, and poking only the top of his head above the surface when he took a breath.

But the biggest of all the dinosaurs was *Brachiosaurus*, whose fossil remains have been found both in North

Brontosaurus

Diplodocus

America and in Africa. His tail was not so long as that of *Diplodocus*, so he measured only about eighty feet. But he was very stout and heavy, and must have weighed about fifty tons, or over eight times as much as a large African elephant of today. A single rib bone was nine feet long.

The front legs of *Brachiosaurus* were unusual because they were longer than the hind legs. This meant that his head was thrust high into the air, on a long heavy neck like that of an overgrown giraffe. His nostrils were on the top of his small head in a little raised dome, so that he could submerge his whole body in the water—except for that small dome—and still breathe comfortably. When he had a little more of his head out of the water, so that his eyes were exposed too, he was like a submarine with a periscope. He could be almost completely hidden in a deep safe pool, and still keep watch for his enemy.

Brontosaurus and his slow, plant-eating relatives survived for about thirty million years, until the Jurassic period ended and the Cretaceous period began. Then the low, marshy sea stretching down into North America began to disappear, and similar seas in other parts of the world receded too. The air became cooler again, and less moist. Many of the plant-eating dinosaurs died at that time. Now paleontologists travel to Wyoming, Utah, and Colorado from all over the world to set up their camps and hunt the fossils of the Jurassic reptiles. Bones and teeth and whole skeletons, carefully dug up from this great "dinosaur cemetery" and exhibited in museums of many lands, have contributed a great deal to man's slowly growing knowledge of the astonishing creatures of the past.

Not all the reptiles that developed before or during the Jurassic period disappeared completely by the end of that time. Two of the groups that continued to survive are particularly interesting to us because their direct descendants are still alive today. In some cases these survivors are almost exactly like their prehistoric ancestors; when we look at them we are seeing creatures that we might have seen if we had lived millions and millions of years ago.

One of these survivors is the odd-looking little tuatara, which makes its home today in just one part of the world —along the rocky coasts of some of the small islands of New Zealand, southeast of Australia. The tuatara is only about 2½ feet long, and has a rather large head and a rather long tail on his small body. His rough skin is a dark

Brachiosaurus

olive green, speckled with white or yellow along the sides, and he has a row of upstanding yellow spines down his back.

The tuatara's prehistoric ancestors looked very much like this modern creature, although some of them were larger and had very long tooth-filled snouts, or beaklike extensions of their jaws. Those ancestors and the little tuatara himself all belong to a group called rhynchocephalians, which means "snout-headed." The rhynchocephalians were apparently never very numerous or very important, but nevertheless they managed to survive longer than most of their ancient neighbors—from the beginning of the long Mesozoic era right up to the present.

Survivors of other ancient reptile groups are our modern crocodiles and alligators, their cousins the gavials, and our modern lizards and snakes.

The first real crocodiles appeared during the Jurassic period, although ancestral animals of the same general family had appeared even earlier. They lived near the water then, just as crocodiles do today. Apparently some ancient crocodiles even ventured into the open sea in search of prey, and one group developed paddlelike feet and lived entirely in the water.

The direct ancestor of modern crocodiles was the rather harmless small reptile called *Eosuchus*, or "true crocodile," who evolved into several larger and more ferocious animals. One of his early descendants was a real giant about fifty feet long. This giant has been called *Phobosuchus*, or "feared crocodile," because he must have been very much feared indeed by his prehistoric neighbors.

Modern descendants of that first little "true crocodile"

are also fearsome, although not so enormous as *Phobosuchus*. They include the crocodile himself, with his long, pointed, dangerous-looking snout. He is found today along the sluggish streams of tropical Africa, Asia, Australia, and America—the same kind of streams that his ancestor inhabited.

The modern alligator, usually smaller than his crocodile cousin, has a broader, shorter snout. Except for one group that lives in China, all modern alligators live in a fairly small area in the United States, from the Gulf of Mexico north to the Carolinas.

Phobosuchus

The third present-day descendant of the first "true crocodile" is the gavial, which is found only in Borneo, Sumatra, India, and other parts of southern Asia. He is the giant of the family, and may grow to a length of thirty feet. His snout is long and pointed, with a queer bump at the tip that he can inflate, or blow up. But in spite of his terrifying and unpleasant looks he is not very dangerous. He has never been known to attack human beings.

One of the strange things about the gavial is his name. The Hindu natives, first to become acquainted with this member of the crocodile family, called him *ghariyal,* which is Hindu for crocodile. The scientist who first wrote about him in English meant to use the Hindu word in a simplified form. He wrote it like this: *garialis.* But the printer could not understand the scientist's handwriting and printed the name as *gavialis.* The mistake was never corrected. Gavialis, or gavial, remains the creature's scientific name to this day.

Modern snakes and modern lizards are both descended from a group of Jurassic-period reptiles which have been named Squamata. The name means "scaly"; the skin of each member of this group is marked off into tiny sections so that it has an uneven, rough, or scaly feeling.

Modern lizards probably bear a close resemblance to ancient reptiles, but they have adapted themselves to all sorts of special environments. The little lizard called a gecko, for example, is completely comfortable in the homes of human beings in Malaya and other Eastern countries. And he is a welcome guest wherever he goes, because he eats hundreds of insects that would otherwise be troublesome to his hosts. He has a small croaking cry which sounds something like "Gecko!" The noise he makes has given him his name.

The little lizard called the chameleon, which is only about six or eight inches long, is protected by the ability of his skin to change its color. When he is climbing up the trunk of a tree he looks brownish or grayish. And when he is among the green leaves, where he usually makes his home, his skin is a greenish color. He moves slowly, but his tongue can dart out as swiftly as lightning to catch an insect. That darting tongue is usually as long as the animal's whole body.

Iguanas and skinks are still other members of the big lizard family, which is not very prominent today but which has managed to endure for millions of years and to survive in climates ranging from very hot to temperate, and from moist to very dry.

Snakes, which are also descendants of ancient reptiles, have evolved in two special ways: they have lost their legs altogether, and their skulls have become very delicate. Few fossils of early snake skulls have ever been found, probably because even the first of these legless reptiles, which developed soon after the close of the Jurassic period, had frail heads like those of modern snakes.

The present-day boa constrictor and the python, both tropical snakes, are probably the most similar to their primitive snake ancestors. And present-day poisonous snakes, wonderfully equipped for the destruction of their enemies, are the most highly specialized descendants of the first snakes.

The smallest of modern snakes and lizards, so unlike their early cousins the giant dinosaurs of the Jurassic period, are interesting examples of the long evolutionary process. They help remind us that not all animals grow larger and larger as they evolve over the centuries, and that it is not always the largest and most powerful creatures that prove to be the ones best fitted for survival.

9 *more dinosaurs*

DURING THE EARLY PART OF THE CRETACEOUS PERIOD, ABOUT 120 million years ago, the earth's face again changed very strikingly. The green plants and trees that had supplied its only color up to that time acquired new and beautiful neighbors. The first flowering plants appeared. By that time there were on earth the bees and other insects that to this day carry pollen from flower to flower. These small winged creatures helped the new plants to spread rapidly.

Other changes were taking place too. While certain dinosaurs disappeared, a few plant eaters not mentioned in the previous chapter did survive, and evolved into important inhabitants of this colorful Cretaceous period. They belonged to the second large group of dinosaurs, the ornithischian or bird-hipped group, whose hip joints were so arranged that the animals usually stood more or less upright on their hind legs.

One member of this group probably survived because

Camptosaurus

he was relatively light and could move around easily. His name was *Camptosaurus*, which means "bent (or flexible) lizard." Specimens of *Camptosaurus* vary in length from seven to seventeen feet. He was probably the first of what became, during the Cretaceous period, a large family of duck-billed plant eaters. He had a rather long low skull, and the front part of his mouth was presumably covered by a horny beak. He could snip off leaves and plants with this beak, just as present-day birds can nip off seeds. All his teeth were set far back in his jaws.

Those jaws, scientists like to point out, closed like a nutcracker, so that the upper and lower rows of teeth came right together. It was a satisfactory arrangement for plant-eating animals. It meant they could chop up their food. And it differed a great deal from the scissorslike jaw pattern of all reptile-hipped dinosaurs, whose jaws slid past each other when they closed. These dinosaurs could not chop up their food. Instead they ripped or tore it. This is one of the most important ways in which the two groups are distinguished from each other.

A close relative of *Camptosaurus* was *Iguanodon*. There is a curious story behind his name. Like the story behind the word dinosaur, it illustrates the great but understandable confusion among early students of prehistoric fossils.

One day in the year 1822 a British paleontologist and

Iguanodon

his wife, Dr. and Mrs. Gideon Mantell, were exploring a bed of fossil remains in southern England. Mrs. Mantell suddenly picked up several teeth, unlike anything her husband had ever seen before. If she had made her discovery fifty years later, when the world was already excited about dinosaurs, the Mantells would probably have been sure that they had found some dinosaur teeth. But in 1822 no one yet knew that those huge animals had ever existed, and when the strange teeth were shown to one of the most famous scientists of the day, that scientist said they belonged to a rhinoceros. But Dr. Mantell was quite sure the expert was wrong, and asked him to study the teeth again. That time the expert decided the teeth had belonged to a hippopotamus.

Dr. Mantell still wasn't satisfied. He looked around further at the place where the teeth had been found, and discovered several strange bones. He fitted the bones together as well as he could, and decided that bones and teeth had all belonged to some animal from the distant past—an animal no living person had ever seen. Because he thought it had probably been about four feet long, and had looked something like the kind of lizard called an iguana, he called his discovery *Iguanodon*.

A good many years passed before scientists learned the real truth about the creature. But finally seventeen complete skeletons were discovered in a Belgian coal mine. These taught the scientists a great deal more than Mantell had been able to learn from his handful of bones. The paleontologists realized that the animal must have been about thirty feet long, with a heavy neck and a thick heavy tail. And the strange pointed bone originally

Stegosaurus

thought to be the tip of the animal's nose proved to be a
sort of pointed thumb on his clawed hand. So in a way
Dr. Mantell had been as wrong as the famous expert who
believed the teeth had belonged to a rhinoceros or a hippopotamus.

But Dr. Mantell remained famous all his life because
he had found at least part of the first dinosaur ever discovered in England. When he died, a plaque was put up
on his house in the village of Lewes. The plaque reads:
He discovered the Iguanodon. The name he invented for
the animal is still used today.

Another bird-hipped creature of the Jurassic period,
Stegosaurus, was also the first representative of a group
that soon became large and prominent. *Stegosaurus* was
the first of the armored reptiles. His name means "cov-

ered lizard," and he wore a double row of heavy stiff triangular plates down his back, covering his backbone. There were also four big sharp spikes at the end of his tail. This handsome armor was not nearly so curious or so effective as that worn by some of his later relatives of the Cretaceous period, but it must have made him outstanding among his completely unarmored Jurassic neighbors.

The duck-billed dinosaurs became numerous early in the Cretaceous period, as shallow seas once more flooded back over low-lying valleys. These dinosaurs had certain traits in common, but they quickly evolved into many strange creatures that were different from each other and different from all other dinosaurs.

All the various members of the duck-billed group spent their time close to the water. Their feet were webbed, so that they didn't sink far into the mud, and their flat bills were useful for snuffling through the ooze of pond bottoms.

Leathery-skinned *Trachodon* looked very much like *Camptosaurus*, his ornithischian ancestor of the Jurassic period. *Trachodon's* heavy tail helped him to balance on his two hind feet and was probably also an advantage when he swam through the water. The most amazing thing about him was his teeth. There were five hundred of them in closely packed rows on each side of his lower jaw and the same number in his upper jaw—a total of two thousand teeth altogether. Each of the four tooth formations made the rough grinding surface that gives the animal his name; the word *Trachodon* means "rough-toothed."

The little town of Haddonfield, New Jersey, has a special interest in this particular dinosaur, just as Dr. Mantell's

Trachodon

village of Lewes has a special interest in *Iguanodon*. Workmen digging near Haddonfield about a century ago noticed some strange bones and told their friends about them. Word spread through the whole town and even to nearby Philadelphia. Sightseers crowded about every day to see the bones and to carry them home as souvenirs. The excitement lasted as long as any bones were to be seen, and then died down as quickly as it had flared up.

But several years later a scientist happened to hear about the bones and went to Haddonfield to see if any more could be found. After a careful search he uncovered more of the huge things. Very much excited, he took them to the famous American paleontologist, Dr. Joseph Leidy, of the University of Pennsylvania. Dr. Leidy was excited

Corythosaurus

too, and soon he was scouring the countryside, trying to
buy up all the souvenir bones people had carried off. He
found some of them being used as doorstops, some of them
on mantel shelves as ornaments. Some he was never able
to find at all. But finally Dr. Leidy pieced together a
partially complete skeleton of rough-toothed *Trachodon*.
It was the first dinosaur skeleton ever found in the United
States.

Many duck-billed dinosaurs were more interesting than
Trachodon, so far as looks were concerned. They had
strange bony formations on their heads which made them
appear to be wearing fancy-dress hats. *Corythosaurus* had
a big rounded crest rising straight up between his eyes.
Lambeosaurus also had a crest, but it flared backward, too,

in a hornlike projection. *Parasaurolophus* had a long slender bone that sprang backward from his forehead like the feather in Robin Hood's cap.

Apparently these duck-bills did not use their bony formations as weapons, but the curious headgear did serve a useful purpose. Some of the animals had especially long air passages, running from their nostrils up through the bony crests. These passages held a great deal of air. *Parasaurolophus*, for example, could take a deep breath,

Parasaurolophus

fill his long air passage, then put his head under water and keep it there for quite a long time before he had to come to the surface again for another supply of oxygen. This meant that he could escape from his enemies simply by rushing into a deep pool, taking a big breath, then submerging himself entirely under the water.

But the shallow seas of the early part of the Cretaceous period slowly subsided. This was the final period of the Mesozoic era, and therefore it saw the slow upsurge and upfolding of new mountains. The great Rocky Mountains, for example, were born at this time. And as the level of the land rose in many areas, pools and marshes and lakes disappeared. Rather dry barren slopes and uplands began to take their place. The areas suitable to the duck-billed dinosaurs were beginning to shrink in size, and the duck-billed population decreased. But new kinds of bird-hipped plant eaters began to evolve, better equipped to survive in the changing climate. They formed a group that has been called the "armored dinosaurs."

Animals that made their homes on waterless plains and uplands were not able to protect themselves from their enemies by hiding in pools, as the duck-bills had done. If they were going to survive at all they had to have some means of defense right at hand, wherever they might be attacked. That's why the plant eaters that developed the best armor were the creatures best able to meet the new conditions of the mid-Cretaceous period.

The most effectively armored successor to *Stegosaurus* —the Jurassic-period reptile that wore a double row of upright plates down his backbone—was *Ankylosaurus*. In

Ankylosaurus

fact he was probably one of the most fully armored animals that ever lived. Scientists have compared him to the big steel tank used in modern warfare, even though *Ankylosaurus* was not very large. He walked on all fours, low and close to the ground. Heavily curved ribs gave him an arched back. Those ribs also gave him his name, which means "curved lizard." His broad skull was covered with bony plates, and his whole arched back was covered with more of these plates, neatly fitted together and heavily knobbed. Along each side, from head to tail, ran a row of sharp outthrusting spikes. And his stiff heavy tail ended in a big solid lump of bone that must have made an excellent club.

But still another group of bird-hipped, plant-eating reptiles was beginning to evolve, and the members of this group outlived even their strongly armored relatives.

Protoceratops

They too were strange-looking creatures, but they were most remarkable for the horns they developed. They have been called the "horned dinosaurs."

Some scientists think that little *Psittacosaurus* of the early Cretaceous period may possibly have been the ancestor of this group. His name means "parrot lizard," and his head looked rather like the head of a parrot, with a narrow skull that ended in a sharp beak. The horned dinosaurs all had a similar sharp-beaked nose.

One of the early horned dinosaurs was *Protoceratops*, only five or six feet long, but so heavy that he had to walk on all fours, as all later members of this group did. His head was large, ending with a parrotlike beak. He did not have a real horn, but he did have a curious bony frill that flared back over his shoulders and extended outward on either side of his eyes. It looked rather like the starched headdress that is part of the native costume in certain European countries. Scientists have discovered that when young *Protoceratops* was first hatched out of his egg his bony frill was relatively very small. It developed slowly, as the animal grew up.

Protoceratops's eggs, incidentally, were the first kind of dinosaur eggs ever to be found. Several nests of them, fossilized and wonderfully preserved, were discovered in Mongolia by paleontologists from the American Museum of Natural History. The eggs are now on display in the big museum in New York City, along with many dinosaur skeletons and other exciting dinosaur exhibits.

A bony frill like that of *Protoceratops* appeared on all the later members of his family, but in each genus it had a special shape. And all the later horned dinosaurs had real horns too.

Styracosaurus

Triceratops

Styracosaurus, for example, had bony spikelike horns extending out from the edge of his bony frill. (*Styracosaurus* means "spike lizard.") He also had a suggestion of two small horns above his eyes, and one large horn that rose almost straight up in the air just above his beaked jaw.

The biggest of the horned dinosaurs was *Triceratops*, whose name means "three-horned face." The single horn above his beak was small, but he had two long sharp ones extending forward over his eyes. His bony frill rose up in a great curve behind them. *Triceratops* was probably about eight feet tall, and measured more than twenty feet from his beak to the tip of his thick heavy tail. His skull alone, ending in that high frill, was eight feet long. And his neck and leg muscles were so powerful that he could lunge forward like a battering ram, thrusting his great horns ahead of him.

Another dinosaur of this time was a strange two-legged creature called *Struthiomimus*, whose ancestors had been meat eaters, but who had developed a taste for other kinds of food. He was probably an egg eater. This animal's name means "ostrich imitator," and he did resemble an ostrich rather closely. His hind legs were long and slender and he had a long ostrichlike neck topped by a toothless, beaked, ostrichlike head. His forelegs were equipped with sharp grasping claws.

Triceratops and *Struthiomimus* probably did not interfere with each other. One moved slowly and ate food close to the ground. The other ran swiftly about and could snatch at eggs in nests.

Triceratops, however, powerful and well armed as he was, did have deadly enemies. These were the great giant meat eaters, the last and most ferocious of the long-lived family of reptile-hipped carnivores called saurischians. Of

Struthiomimus

Tyrannosaurus

these, *Tyrannosaurus*, or "tyrant lizard," may well have been the mightiest, most terrifying land animal in the history of the world.

He was enormous. His great heavy body reared twenty feet above the ground on its hind legs, balanced on two huge clawed feet and a massive tail. From tip of head to tip of tail he measured some forty-seven feet. His forearms were tiny and useless-looking, but *Tyrannosaurus* did not depend on them as weapons. The only weapon he needed was his enormous pair of jaws, set with rows of great teeth. Each tooth was like a curved dagger—a six-inch-long fang ending in a sharp point.

Tyrannosaurus had a giant's strength to match his giant size. He must have been more terrifying than any fairy-tale ogre or any legendary dragon. When his huge mouth gaped open and then closed down on a victim, that single tearing, crushing attack must have meant certain death.

While *Tyrannosaurus* stalked the earth, few other living creatures were safe. All smaller meat eaters had to keep watch for the giant's approach, while they themselves sought still smaller animals to eat. And among the plant eaters probably only horned *Triceratops* and heavily armored *Ankylosaurus* could expect to survive an assault by the fearsome monster.

Every period of history is a battle for survival. Plant eaters have always had to struggle for their lives against meat eaters, and small meat eaters have had to struggle against larger ones. But perhaps the battle that raged over the earth during the Cretaceous period, as the great Mesozoic era was coming to a close, was the most bloody and ferocious the world has ever seen.

That battle came to an end as the Mesozoic era itself ended, and the Cenozoic—the era that stretches up to our present time—began. Scientists are not sure why this happened. They only know that within a span of several million years—a brief interval, as paleontologists reckon time—*Triceratops* and his relatives vanished, and their huge enemies vanished too, including great *Tyrannosaurus* himself.

Several explanations have been offered for this amazing disappearance, but none of them seems completely satisfactory. It is likely, for example, that plants were becoming scarcer in the severe climate at the end of the period, and that plant eaters began to perish for lack of food. As they perished, of course, there was less food for the animals who lived on the plant eaters' flesh, and so many of the meat eaters probably starved to death too. But scientists know that the world did not become completely barren at that time. Many areas remained green and moist enough to provide food for at least some members of the family to which *Triceratops* belonged. And so long as any of those creatures were left, there seems no reason why their enemies should not have continued to survive too.

Another explanation points out that all the dinosaurs had extremely small and primitive brains. Thirty-five-ton *Brontosaurus*, for example, had a brain that weighed only a few ounces, almost nothing as compared to the ten-pound brain of a modern elephant. Some people say that dinosaurs were just too stupid to adapt themselves to changing conditions. But there are strong arguments against this explanation.

For one thing, every dinosaur had a nerve center in his spinal cord, near the hip joint. This nerve center controlled the movements of his hind legs and his tail— movements which in modern animals are controlled by the brain itself. So the dinosaur's brain didn't need to be large enough to contain the nerve centers that controlled his whole body.

It is probably true that dinosaurs couldn't reason. But they had been able to "muddle through life," as one scientist puts it, for many millions of years. And, as a group, they had shown a remarkable adaptability. Over and over again they had evolved into new varieties to meet new conditions. The herbivores, for example, at a time when the inland seas were shrinking, had evolved from water-loving, water-protected animals into animals that were protected by their own armor. And they had evolved again into horned creatures who could actively fight off the attacks of their enemies. So it is not enough to say that they were stupid. They had always been stupid, but their stupidity had never before prevented them from adapting to an ever-changing world.

Apparently there is no one single explanation that completely answers the question, "Why did the dinosaurs become extinct?" Perhaps each explanation gives a part of the answer, but even all of them together do not make up a very satisfactory reply. For the present, at least, the question indicates one of the still-unsolved mysteries in the story of prehistoric animals.

Many people used to say that although the dinosaurs were the biggest land creatures that ever lived, they were failures just the same, else they never would have become extinct.

But scientists have proved that this was a foolish remark for any human being to have made. Modern human beings, after all, have probably existed for only about fifty thousand years, according to the most recent scientific calculations. And nobody knows how much longer human beings will continue to exist—how well they will be able to go on adapting themselves to an ever-changing world. So it is only fair to remember that the dinosaurs, even though they did finally become extinct, had existed and ruled the earth for about 120 million years—2,400 times as long as the period of man's whole existence up to now!

10 *swimming and flying reptiles*

THE DINOSAURS WERE NOT THE ONLY REPTILES THAT ESTAB-
lished themselves as mighty rulers during the Mesozoic
period. While they were becoming lords of the land,
other reptiles were returning to the water, the ancestral
home of all living things, to become for a time the un-
disputed tyrants of the sea. And still other reptiles were
taking over the third and remaining realm—the realm of
the air.

The Mesozoic era was, in fact—in the sea and in the air,
as well as on the land—the great Age of Reptiles.

There were four principal groups of reptiles that returned to the water.

One of those groups was quite closely related to the
dinosaurs, and also to the little "true crocodile," the ancestor of the modern crocodile and his relatives. For this
reason the members of this group, scientifically known
as geosaurs, are sometimes called "marine crocodiles."
Their bodies became long and flexible, so that they could

Mosasaur

propel themselves easily through the water, and their four limbs evolved into flat paddles. They thrust themselves along with the help of their tails.

The second group that returned to the water, the mosasaurs, were also related to the dinosaurs, but not so closely. Their name, which means "Meuse lizards," was given to them because their first fossil remains were found near the Meuse River in Europe.

The mosasaurs are sometimes called sea lizards, and that is exactly what they were—lizards who adapted themselves to life in the water, and who flourished so successfully there that they became the giants of the sea. The biggest of all mosasaurs was *Tylosaurus*, whose powerful, sharp-jawed body was more than twenty feet long.

But the third and fourth groups—the plesiosaurs and their relatives, and the ichthyosaurs—were of more im-

Ichthyosaur

portance than either the sea lizards or the sea crocodiles.

The streamlined, medium-sized ichthyosaurs, which swarmed through the seas during the Triassic period, really looked very much like fish. They probably evolved from small primitive reptiles like the mesosaurs, which had long sharp jaws, thin necks, and paddlelike feet, and which returned to the water even before the dawn of the Mesozoic era. As time went by, the feet became more like paddles, the narrow tail broadened into the fan-shaped tail of a fish, the neck disappeared, and the whole body became sleek and torpedo-shaped. An ichthyosaur, in other words, really deserved his name, which means "fish lizard." He even acquired a big upstanding fin on his back, which helped to balance him as he moved through the water.

One reason the ichthyosaur is interesting is that its eggs remained inside the female's body until they hatched, so that the mother gave birth to live young. The scientific way to describe this unusual characteristic is to say that the ichthyosaur was ovoviviparous. Any creature that lays eggs is called oviparous, from the Latin word *ovum* which means "egg," and the Latin word *parere* which means "to bring forth." Any creature that gives birth to live young is called viviparous. The first part of that word comes from the Latin *vivus*, which means "alive." So the word ovoviviparous shows that this strange water reptile had its own strange method: it did produce eggs, but actual birth took place after the eggs had hatched into living young inside the reptile's body.

Another reason scientists are especially interested in the ichthyosaur is that he shows how the process of evolution sometimes appears to move in a circle. The ichthyosaur was the final form of original sea dwellers who first evolved into amphibians, living half in the water and half on land, then into true land-dwelling reptiles, and then back again into fishlike sea dwellers.

But the ichthyosaur was not really a fish after all. His skeleton was that of a reptile, and he breathed with lungs and not with fishlike gills. He had come to look like a fish only because he lived as fishes do. Scientists call him an "imitation fish," an example of what they call "convergence." Convergence occurs when two separate lines of evolution seem to converge—to produce animals which look alike, even though they retain the basic features of their own group. Convergence has occurred more than once in the long history of evolution.

The most important member of the fourth group of water-dwelling reptiles—the plesiosaur, or "near lizard"— was also an imitator. He looked rather like a turtle or, as

Plesiosaur

someone once said, like "a snake strung through the body of a turtle." His body was broad and flat, and he probably paddled along close beneath the surface of the water with his long, oarlike, finny feet. But his head, with its sharp-toothed jaws, stuck out at the end of a longish neck, so that he could snap swiftly at passing fish.

The first plesiosaur skeleton and the first ichthyosaur skeleton ever found were both discovered by a young girl named Mary Anning, who was born in the year 1799 in the little English seacoast village of Lyme Regis. She was just twelve years old when she found the ichthyosaur skeleton, but it made her famous throughout the whole scientific world.

Even at the age of twelve, however, Mary was not just an amateur fossil collector. The countryside around her village was rich in fossil shells, and Mary's father had taken her fossil hunting ever since she was very small. The science of paleontology was still undeveloped in those days, but people were already collecting all sorts of fossils as souvenirs, to arrange on shelves and in curio cabinets. Mary's father, who was a cabinetmaker by trade, had learned that he could add to his income by collecting fossil shells and selling them to the well-to-do people who visited little Lyme Regis for the swimming and the sea air.

When Mary found a complete skeleton one day—the skeleton of a strange, unknown creature, for which scientists invented the name ichthyosaur—she became more interested than ever in fossil hunting. She went on collecting shells, of course, but always hoped that some day she would find another curious skeleton. And she did. In 1821 she found the plesiosaur skeleton, and from then on fossil hunting became her real business.

She studied rock-strata formations, so that she would know the most likely places to look for specimens. She learned how to dig up fragile skeletons without injuring or disarranging the bones. And she learned how to preserve her finds so that they would be most useful to the increasing number of scientists who were making a study of prehistoric creatures. Wealthy collectors and museum representatives came regularly to Lyme Regis to look at Mary's discoveries, and she always had eager customers for the remarkable number of finds she made during her lifetime.

In 1828 Mary Anning made the third of her three most important discoveries. She found the first skeleton ever seen in England of a creature which looked very much like a lizard, but which had real batlike wings. The animal was named pterosaur, or "winged reptile," and it made scientists aware of a whole new reptile family—the family of reptiles which had taken to the air.

Since that time scientists have learned that there were really two groups of reptiles which developed wings. One group, the pterosaurs, became extinct at the end of the Mesozoic era, when their land relatives, the dinosaurs, and their other relatives, the water-dwelling reptiles, also disappeared. The second group evolved into all the birds that live on the earth today.

The pterosaur whose skeleton Mary Anning found probably looked rather like a modern bat, although he was not really a member of the bat family. Scientists don't yet know his full story, but they think it began in the Jurassic period. At that time, according to other fossil skeletons discovered after Mary Anning made her dramatic find, there existed a small lizardlike creature called *Rhamphorhynchus*, or "prow-beaked reptile." His body was scarcely bigger than a fist, but he had a long tail and long beak-shaped jaws with sharp teeth. His bones were hollow and thus very light, and they were fitted snugly together so that he was strong and sturdy. He could control his small body remarkably well, too. His nervous system had become so well developed that he had a good sense of balance.

But his front hands were the most startling thing about him. On each hand the fourth finger had become enor-

Rhamphorhynchus

mously long—as long as the animal's whole body. And stretching from the tip of this finger, along the animal's arm and down to his body, was a light membrane, like the webbing between the toes of a duck's foot. When the animal lifted his arms, this skin stretched into a thin, taut wing.

Probably this creature couldn't really fly. If he was on the ground, he probably couldn't flap his wings and lift himself into the air. But if he climbed a tree, clinging to the bark with his sharp claws, and leaped from a high branch, his wings would let him come gently earthward in a long glide.

The pterosaur skeleton which Mary Anning found showed that by the Cretaceous period this little gliding

Pteranodon

reptile had lost some of his lizardlike characteristics and evolved into a real giant of the air. He no longer had teeth in his long beaklike jaws, and his tail had nearly disappeared. His body itself had not changed very much and it was still quite small. But those long fingers had grown even longer, and the wings had grown with them. Now they measured more than twenty feet from tip to outstretched tip.

The big pterosaur *Pteranodon* was probably a glider too, and not a real flier. But it seems likely that he learned how to soar with rising air currents, and how to drift along with light winds, so perhaps he was able to travel long distances through the air. Scientists know that he had a very poor sense of smell, so that he wasn't equipped to sniff along the ground in search of food. His hind legs were weak too, so he probably couldn't move over the ground quickly or for very long at a time. Scientists also know that he had large eyes and probably very good vision. They think this means that he sighted his prey from the air, as hawks do today, and glided down to snatch it up in his claws. And if he did all his food hunting from the air, scientists say, he must have spent most of his time swooping about overhead. He was a real dweller in the air.

The flying reptile existed for more than fifty million years. So he was apparently as well equipped to survive in the latter part of the Mesozoic era as the big dinosaurs were. But, like the dinosaurs, he disappeared at the end of that era too, perhaps because of competition with the birds.

By the year 1861 the science of paleontology was growing up. By studying fossils of all kinds and arranging them in order according to the rock strata where they had been found, men had learned a great deal about the ancient life of the earth. They knew something about the dinosaurs and many of the other strange members of the great reptile family that populated most of the world during the whole Mesozoic era. Many scientists had accepted as a guide the theory of evolution which Darwin had just published. They had already come to believe, for example, that the first reptiles had evolved from amphibians, and that the early reptiles in turn had evolved into dinosaurs, and into modern lizards and crocodiles and other creatures. In other words they had learned to trace, from the fossils in one layer of rock to the fossils in another, the history of many of the earth's past and present inhabitants.

But of course there were still many mysteries which had not yet been solved. One of the most puzzling of all was the origin of all the birds in the world.

Where had birds come from? And when had they first appeared on the earth? In 1861 nobody could answer those questions. But almost all scientists felt quite sure that there had not been any birds at all on the earth until some time after the end of the Mesozoic era. All the bird fossils they had ever found were in rock layers formed later than that time.

Some people said that birds appeared on the earth very suddenly and not by evolving from some earlier kind of animal. They claimed that Darwin's whole theory was wrong and that each group of animals appeared on the earth by itself, fully formed, and not by evolution.

Scientists disagreed with this idea and in the year 1861, while this argument was going on, a strange thing happened. In a limestone quarry in Germany, in a stratum of rock that all scientists agreed had been formed in the Jurassic period of the Mesozoic era, workmen found a nearly complete fossil skeleton that amazed the whole world. The bones were certainly the bones of a reptile, the experts thought. The animal had had a tail, and it had had claws on its feet. But it had also had real feathered wings! The imprint of the feathers was very clearly preserved in the smooth stone.

The scientists who believed in the theory of evolution were very much excited. To them this discovery proved that birds evolved from an earlier form of life—in other words, from reptiles. They named the fossil animal *Archaeopteryx*, or "ancient winged creature," and declared he was half reptile and half bird—a sort of halfway mark between ancient reptiles and modern birds.

Today most scientists agree with them. They believe that in the Mesozoic era certain small reptiles with strong hind legs somehow developed the art of flying. Perhaps they began by running swiftly over the ground on their hind legs and flapping their forelegs, until after millions

Archaeopteryx

of years these flapping motions became real flying motions, and the creatures could actually lift themselves off the ground. Or perhaps they began by gliding. To this day nobody knows how the first feathers developed. Scientists know that a thick skin sometimes evolved into a scaly skin, and they say that feathers are really "highly modified scales." But they admit there is a big gap between scaly skin and real feathers, and they don't know how that gap was bridged. It is one more of the still unsolved mysteries of the past.

Fossil discoveries during the past seventy-five years have proved that by the end of the Mesozoic era several kinds of birds had developed. Some became as much at home in the water as modern ducks. Others were ground-walking birds, like the modern ostrich. Their wings were too small to lift them into the air; and they stalked about on hind legs that were sometimes as long and awkward as an ostrich's legs. *Phororhacos*, one of the biggest of these

Phororhacos

early ground birds, had a huge beak and a head as large
as the head of a horse.

But the early water birds did not survive very long.
And most of the early ground birds died out after a time
too, probably because they had so many four-footed en-

emies and so many rivals for food. One strange example, the tiny-winged, fat-bodied dodo bird, did survive in Australia until the seventeenth century. Then he, too, finally disappeared.

The dodo doesn't really deserve to be called a prehistoric animal, because he lived far into our own present period. He is a part of recorded history. He is, however, an extinct animal—one that no longer exists at all. He had fallen prey to a superior animal, modern man. When people first realized that this bird had actually disappeared from the earth, they were surprised at this striking illustration of the theory of evolution taking place almost under their eyes. The phrase, "dead as a dodo," became very popular, useful for describing anything that was completely finished, that had proved itself unable to survive.

Other early birds were small and spent most of the time aboveground, in the air or in the trees. They were safe there, and had the opportunity to thrive and develop.

Their wings were much sturdier than the weblike wings of the gliding reptile pterosaur. If the pterosaur's wing became torn, he was helpless. But a bird could lose or break a feather or two and still fly. Furthermore a bird's wing was not attached to a single finger, like the wing of a pterosaur. The bird's finger bones, light but strong like all the bones in its body, had grown together. And its feathers were attached not only to this unified framework, but also to the whole lower part of its arm. The powerful wing muscles were attached to a breastbone that had become large enough to give them plenty of support.

Many birds developed the habit of building nests, so

that their eggs were protected and their young could be cared for until they were ready and old enough to fly. This was another reason birds were able to survive.

A third reason was that birds had acquired warm blood in place of the cold blood of their reptile ancestors. No one knows why or how this blood change took place, but it was certainly very important. A warm-blooded animal can withstand severe changes of temperature and can be active for a long period of time without becoming exhausted. Chapter 11 explains more about the value of this development.

Today there are thousands of kinds of birds in the world. There are dozens of varieties of warblers alone, for example, each one an offshoot, or specialized descendant, of some prehistoric warblerlike ancestor. In fact, birds are the most numerous and most important descendants of the ancient reptiles who ruled the whole world for so long, and who finally lost their land empire and their sea kingdom. Today only lizards, crocodiles, and a few other members of the once proud reptile family continue to struggle for existence on earth and in the water. But the air is alive with the feathered descendants of the first winged reptiles.

They lead a useful life, supplying food to man, distributing seeds from place to place, and destroying harmful insects. They fill the world with the music of their song and the color of their plumage. They are the richest and most amazing legacy left to our own time by that ancient and giant-crowded time known as the Age of Reptiles.

11   *the first mammals*

BACK IN THE DISTANT JURASSIC PERIOD, IN THE TIME OF the gigantic dinosaurs, it might have seemed that no other living creature could ever threaten their superiority. But even while huge *Tyrannosaurus* and his relatives were terrorizing the earth there were tiny animals living in trees, in holes, and under logs and stones, who would one day take over the authority of the dinosaurs.

These obscure little creatures were the mammals, a group which began to dominate the earth about sixty or seventy million years ago, and is still dominant to this day. Man himself, the present-day earth ruler, belongs to this ancient and amazing group.

Certainly the earliest mammals were no match for their reptile neighbors in either size or strength. Few were larger than a rat, and probably they seldom dared to emerge from their safe hiding places until after dark. Yet they managed to cling to life in spite of the dangers that surrounded them. They watched the great dinosaurs decrease in number and finally vanish entirely. Then for the first time they could safely come down from the trees and out of their holes and explore in broad daylight the great world they had inherited.

Probably the mammals were able to survive until that moment, and were able to hold the position of leadership they acquired, because they differed from the reptiles in so many ways. For one thing they give birth to their children by a method very different from that of the reptiles. Reptiles lay eggs, usually in a shallow hole on the open ground. Eggs are often stolen and eaten before they have a chance to hatch. Even if the reptile eggs are not eaten, the life inside them may be destroyed by severe heat or cold. And in any case newborn reptile babies, left to fend for themselves, don't always live to grow up.

Most mammals, on the other hand, don't lay eggs at all. They give birth to living babies instead. And the mother doesn't just wander off and leave the newborn babies to look after themselves, as reptile mothers do. She guards them and feeds them milk until they are old enough to find their own food, and to know their enemies and defend themselves.

Mammals differ from reptiles in another important way. Reptiles are cold-blooded animals: their body temperature changes with the temperature of the air around them. On a hot day a reptile is overheated and sluggish and moves as little as possible. On a cold day he is also sluggish and may scarcely move at all. Both extremes of weather make it difficult for him to find food, and a reptile sometimes dies of heat or cold. Scientists think this cold-blooded condition may have been another reason why the dinosaurs finally became extinct.

But mammals are warm-blooded: their bodies stay at about the same temperature on hot days and cold. Like a car motor that is not allowed to become overheated or to freeze, a mammal can perform efficiently in all kinds of weather. Most mammals have hairy or furry coats that further protect them against the cold, in a way no reptile was ever protected. These warm coats certainly helped some of them to live through the great Ice Age.

Other important differences between reptiles and mammals can be seen in the bone and muscle structure of the two kinds of animals, and in their teeth. Mammals' skeletons are much better designed for quick action than reptiles' are, and mammals can keep on the move much longer without tiring. This must have been a great advantage to the early members of the family at the time when hungry reptiles threatened them from every side.

Mammals also have jaws that move sideways, as well as with the up-and-down motion of the reptiles' jaws. And their three kinds of teeth—sharp ones in front, broad chewing teeth in back, and daggerlike canine or dog teeth on either side—make it possible for them to eat almost anything. The earliest mammals didn't have to risk their lives searching far and wide for one certain kind of food. They could peel bark from trees, or slash through the tough shell of a nut, or snap up an insect. And their strong back teeth could grind and chew up whatever they found.

Scientists are fairly certain that the mammals did not

acquire all these advantages at once, although the experts do not know very much about the earliest members of the group because their fossils are so rare. Nevertheless, a few early mammal fossils have been found on every continent except Australia and Antarctica, so these little animals apparently were able to live in almost every corner of the earth.

Most of the mammal fossils that date from the Mesozoic era, the Age of Reptiles, are jawbones or teeth. That is why scientists usually classify these early, or Mesozoic, mammals according to the kind of teeth they had. One group appears as far back as the Jurassic period. It has been named the multituberculate group, because the molars of the teeth had parallel rows of tubercles, or cusps. The first multituberculates were small, rodentlike animals that probably laid eggs instead of giving birth to live young. (A few mammals—the platypus of Australia is one—do that even to this day.)

The multituberculates were the first herbivorous mammals, and flourished from the Jurassic all through the Paleocene epoch. Some species evolved, as time went by, into much larger creatures such as *Taeniolabis*. *Taeniolabis*, which was probably covered with fur and had whiskers, was about as large as a beaver and had a head something like that of a modern woodchuck.

The most important Jurassic group of mammals, however, was one called the pantotheres. They were numerous and varied during the Jurassic period, then appear to have died out, but scientists believe them to be the true ancestors of all the mammal types that followed and even of the ones we know today.

Remains of mammals of the Jurassic period, excepting the multituberculates, show them as small animals probably somewhat like rats and mice in size and appearance. Most of them probably ate insects, but supplemented this diet with fruit or eggs. They were very primitive creatures, but there is indirect evidence that at least some of them may already have nursed their young and possibly may have borne them alive.

Fossils from the next period, the Cretaceous—still in the Age of Reptiles—show that multituberculates still flourished and that descendants of the pantotheres had already developed into the two great groups of mammals still existing today: marsupials and placentals. Almost all marsupials carry their prematurely born young in external pouches until the infants develop sufficiently to fend for themselves. The kangaroo, which lives only in Australia, and the opossum of the Western Hemisphere are among the best known of modern marsupials. In the Cretaceous period, many opossumlike marsupials seem to have lived in

Thylacodon

North America. *Thylacodon* was an early member of this long-lived family which still exists today.

The placentals are animals who carry their young internally and give birth to them at a much more advanced stage than do the marsupials. Although they were not nearly so abundant during the Cretaceous period as were the marsupials, they were better adapted to life, with more efficient brains and bodies, and in time they outstripped the marsupials. Almost all mammals of today are placentals.

The early placentals seem to have been insect eaters like their Jurassic ancestors. They had teeth and jaws especially suited for eating insects. These primitive insect eaters, or insectivores, as they are called, looked something like our present-day shrew. Probably most of them were very small, too. One member of the family had a skull only about an inch long. Scientists consider forms of insectivores living today, such as the shrews, moles, and hedgehogs, the most direct descendants of the earliest placentals.

The real Age of Mammals began in the Paleocene epoch—the first epoch of our present or Cenozoic era. Conditions in this epoch were wonderfully suited to the development of the small and defenseless mammals. They were no longer in danger from creatures much larger than themselves. The climate was becoming mild and pleasant and there was plenty of food. They began to multiply rapidly, and many new groups soon appeared.

Two of the most important new groups were the creodonts and the condylarths. All the animals in both groups originally looked rather alike, although they ranged from the size of a rat to that of a dog. In general their heads were rather doglike, but more blunt, and their ears were quite small. Their long thick tails tapered to a point and their short thick legs ended in five-toed feet. But the toes on those feet were rather strange: they ended in something that was not a real claw and not a real hoof; it might some day evolve either into sharp claws for digging and slashing, or into hoofs adapted for swift running.

Although both the creodonts and the condylarths could probably eat all kinds of food, a few creodonts already preferred meat, and the condylarths generally preferred green leaves and plants. Scientists think they may therefore have been very distant ancestors of modern claw-footed meat eaters such as wolves and lions, and modern hoofed plant eaters such as horses and cows.

But while creodonts were prowling around seeking meat to satisfy their growing carnivorous appetites, and while condylarths were chewing leaves and shoots, an animal of still another group was climbing around in the trees at night. This small creature probably looked something like a modern lemur, and has been named *Plesiadapis*, which means "nearly like a lemur." Perhaps he wasn't very prominent in his own day, but he is interesting because he introduces us for the first time to a newly evolved group of mammals called the primates, which would eventually become very large and important. Modern primates, distant relatives of that little *Plesiadapis*, include not only the lemurs—monkeylike animals with foxlike heads—but monkeys themselves and apes and men.

Slowly, as the centuries passed, some mammals continued to increase in size. By the end of the Paleocene

Pantolambda

epoch one creature had appeared that was as big as a
sheep, and another that was even larger. Both were plant
eaters and both belonged to a group called amblypods,
which survived for millions of years before they finally
became extinct. All amblypods—the name means "slow-
footed"—were hoofed animals, which scientists call ungulates. Each of their five toes ended in a small hoof.

The sheep-sized animal, named *Pantolambda*, had a
long tail and a long slender body. And since these two
characteristics often appear in cats, which are meat eaters,
scientists think there must have been some meat eaters
among *Pantolambda's* ancestors.

The second new large animal, *Barylambda*, sometimes
grew to a length of eight feet and was the giant of his day.
His body was long and heavy, with a strong, bulky tail.
But his head, with ears set far back, was very small for
such a big body. And his five hoofed toes were on broad
but very short feet. He probably had to move slowly and
awkwardly through the lush forests of the late Paleocene

epoch and other animals may not have feared him even if he was so much bigger than they were.

Small, squirrel-like *Paramys*, which also appeared during that epoch, was a very early representative of another important group of mammals: the rodents. Modern squirrels, along with other gnawing animals such as rats, mice, rabbits, and beavers, all belong to this group.

By the time the Paleocene epoch drew to a close the mammals were probably very numerous, and there were certainly many groups of them, each group differing from the rest. Yet the differences were not as sharp as they would become later. Animals that were mostly plant eaters, or herbivores, for example, still shared certain features with the carnivores. And few animals had what we now think of as real hoofs or real claws. Instead they had hooflike claws or clawlike hoofs. Though as a group they were

Barylambda

Paramys

the ancestors of modern dogs and cats, horses and cows, no Paleocene mammals really looked very much like a dog or a cat, a horse or a cow. When scientists describe those early creatures, they seldom can make any more definite statement than that a certain animal had a catlike body or a doglike head.

By the time the Paleocene epoch ended, in other words, the recognizable ancestors of most of today's mammals were still a long way in the future. But the mammals had nevertheless evolved considerably during that first ten-million-year period when they were free to roam the earth unterrified by creatures much larger than themselves. And they were to evolve even more dramatically during the Eocene epoch which followed.

12 *the mammals multiply*

THE GENERALLY WARM AND PLEASANT CLIMATE OF THE
Paleocene epoch continued through the Eocene, and the
vegetation of the world thrived. This, of course, guaran-
teed a plentiful supply of food for all plant eaters, and
they multiplied and evolved into new types of animals.
And since a large plant-eating population naturally pro-
vides a good food supply for meat eaters, the carnivorous
animals also became more numerous and branched out
into new species.

The hoofed amblypods, for example—the group that
included comparatively big *Barylambda*—now produced
the even bigger *Coryphodon*. This awkward creature was
as large as a hippopotamus and just about as slow and
ungainly. On huge flat five-toed feet not unlike those of a
modern elephant he lumbered about among the trees,
eating soft shoots and green leaves. But though his den-
tal equipment was chiefly suitable for this kind of food,
he also had large canine teeth almost tusklike in size and
shape.

Coryphodon

His weird-looking contemporaries *Uintatherium* and *Eobasileus* were even larger than *Coryphodon*. Sometimes they grew to the size of a rhinoceros and they too had huge flat elephantlike feet. But it was their long heads, topped by hornlike bumps, that gave them their weird appearance. Those bumps, which scientists think were skin-covered bones rather than real horns, were arranged in pairs. Each of the two animals wore his foremost pair over the nose, his second pair in front of the eyes, and his third pair just in front of the ears. And each also had, in addition to these weapons, long tusks that grew downward out of his upper jaws.

These two amblypods were probably the largest herbivores of their day, and probably few meat eaters dared to attack them.

Plant-eating *Phenacodus*, on the other hand—one of the new members of the big condylarth group—probably had to depend on speed in order to escape from his enemies.

His long thick tail seemed too big for his body, which might be the size of a sheep or the size of a fox. There were small ears on his rather long head, and a pair of fairly long dog teeth in his small jaws. His five-toed feet ended in hoofs rather than claws, but they looked rather like a dog's feet, and apparently *Phenacodus* could run well enough, but clumsily.

Another new plant eater, *Palaeosyops*, had such well-developed dog teeth that he could probably use them as defensive weapons, but in other respects he must have been rather defenseless. His smallish body, with its amazingly horselike head, stood on rather slender legs. There were four toes on his front feet and only three toes on his hind feet. Little *Palaeosyops* appeared in great numbers during the Eocene epoch, then later became extinct. But the group he belonged to, called the titanotheres, survived for a long time and some members of it eventually evolved into ponderous giants. Probably that is why scientists gave

Eobasilius

the whole group its curious name, titanotheres, which means "gigantic little beasts."

Some of the Eocene plant eaters are particularly interesting to a scientific detective because, unlike most earlier mammals, they can be clearly recognized as ancestors of modern plant eaters. In fact this period produced the first recognizable members of four great present-day families: horses, camels, rhinoceroses, and elephants. Usually, of course, nobody but an expert can see the resemblance between the prehistoric mammal and its modern descendant, but the resemblance is there in every case. It can be traced by many clues in the teeth and skeleton.

Little eohippus, of the Eocene epoch, although he was scarcely larger than a big house cat or a fox, has been identified as a very early member of the horse family. That is why he was given his name, which means "dawn

Uintatherium

Eohippus

horse." His feet, four-toed in front and three-toed in back, looked nothing at all like a modern horse's feet. But there was something definitely horselike about his small body, and his long head had a rather horsy shape—though perhaps no more so than the head of that un-related animal, *Palaeosyops*. Like other plant eaters of his day, eohippus had teeth adapted for eating leaves and shoots.

Protylopus, another small Eocene mammal about the size of a jackrabbit, with a rather long head and short limbs, has been recognized by the scientists as a very early camel, in spite of the fact that he had no hump.

A slender-headed animal called *Hyrachyus*, which varied in height from two to four feet and which had no horns at all, is now regarded as a very early member of the great rhinoceros family.

And scientists say the first member of the elephant family was pig-sized *Moeritherium* of the Eocene epoch. He had no trunk and no tusks. In fact he looked no more like a modern elephant than *Hyrachyus* looked like a modern rhinoceros. His habits were different from those of a modern elephant, too. Fossil remains of this creature,

Hyrachyus

found in beds of mud laid down in Egypt, suggest that he may have liked to wallow in shallow muddy water.

But in some ways the structure of each of these animals suggests, to expert paleontologists at least, that the first ancestors of the horse, the camel, the rhinoceros, and the elephant had made their appearance on the earth. And slowly, after millions of years, these small primitive creatures would evolve into animals more closely resembling the modern members of their families.

The Eocene mammals mentioned so far were plant eaters, but naturally they shared the world of their day with their enemies the meat eaters. All the meat eaters of this period belonged to the creodont family, the primitive carnivores that had already become numerous during the earlier Paleocene epoch. Many of these creodonts were completely unlike anything to be seen on the earth today, but others would not seem strange to us because they look rather like modern cats or dogs or weasels.

But a prehistoric animal with, for example, a catlike body, may have had no connection with modern cats at all; instead he may have been an ancestral member of the modern dog family. And prehistoric animals closely resembling a modern dog may have changed in later generations so that they eventually became what is called the short-faced bear family. Only the discovery and study of more and more fossils will finally make clear the many complicated steps by which Eocene mammals became the mammals of the present day.

Three of the more common creodonts of the Eocene

Moeritherium

epoch were little doglike *Mesonyx,* slinky weasel-like *Tritemnodon,* and fierce *Patriofelis,* which had a catlike head and a long catlike tail. But the most outstanding members of the group were probably the giant called *Sarkastodon* and his even larger relative *Andrewsarchus.*

Sarkastodon looked rather catlike, but he had fangs as thick and powerful as those of a grizzly bear. And great wolflike *Andrewsarchus,* with a head more than three feet long, would have dwarfed even the huge modern Kodiak bear, which is the largest meat eater in the world today. *Andrewsarchus* was, so far as scientists now know, the biggest meat-eating land mammal that ever lived.

But while these large and small creodonts were roaming the earth, other mammal groups were steadily evolving toward creatures that exist today. The rodent group,

Mesonyx

Patriofelis

for example, which began to flourish in the Paleocene epoch, now consisted of many different kinds of small, long-tailed creatures with sharp teeth very useful for gnawing. Most of them probably bore a close resemblance to little squirrel-like *Paramys*, that primitive rodent which still survived from the earlier period.

And the primates, represented earlier by lemur-like *Plesiadapis*, now also appeared in greater numbers. The members of this group had not yet grown in size, however, as they would do later. Little *Notharctus*, for example, had a foxlike head only a few inches long. Probably he lived on nuts, fruits, and insects, and spent most of his life in the safety of the treetops. His distant relative *Tetonius*,

Notharctus

equally small, had such enormous eyes that scientists think he used them mostly in the dark, and remained snugly out of sight of his meat-eating neighbors all during the day.

In this period, too, one new group appeared which would eventually evolve into modern anteaters, sloths, and armadillos. These were the edentates. The word edentate means "toothless," and though some members of this group did have teeth of a sort, these were usually scarce and fairly useless. One of the earliest edentates, *Metacheiromys*, had two canine teeth, although scientists think he may also have had in his mouth horny pads with which he ground up his leafy diet. He was over a foot long, but stood only four inches high and may have looked something like a squat modern armadillo.

Before the Eocene epoch came to an end, the earth-ruling mammals—like the reptiles before them, in the era when they ruled the world—had extended their domain into the air and into the sea. They had acquired wings. And they had evolved into new varieties of "imitation fish" which had returned to the water to live and had begun to look very much like their neighbors, the true fish, though they still kept all the most important characteristics of mammals.

The new winged mammals were the ancestors of all modern bats. They never grew as large as the largest

Tetonius

Seal

flying reptiles; even today a bat with a wing spread of five feet is unusual. But bats' weblike wings, supported by several fingers instead of by a single finger, are stronger and less easily torn than were flying reptiles' wings. And bats have developed remarkably acute senses of touch and hearing which make them quickly aware of obstacles looming in their path. Their huge ears are usually the most noticeable feature of their tiny heads. Probably it was because of their specialized physical development that they were able to survive instead of becoming extinct.

Today there are bats in almost every part of the world, and they have evolved into numerous kinds, including the small common grayish bat that clings almost invisibly to grayish tree trunks, and the brilliant orange-furred bat that lives only in India and Malaya. Most bats eat insects or fruit, but the variety called "vampire" lives by sucking the blood of living cattle and other animals.

Whatever their looks and habits, however, all bats are mammals. They are warm-blooded furry creatures that give birth to live young and nurse them.

The mammals that returned to the ancestral home of all animals, the sea, became the ancestors of such modern sea creatures as seals and walruses, dolphins, porpoises, and whales.

Walrus

The mammals who first went back to the sea were probably, in the beginning, rather wolflike meat eaters that simply lived close to the shore and became accustomed to a diet of fish and shellfish instead of ordinary meat. Then, perhaps at a time when their enemies were particularly numerous or food in the water was particularly abundant, they began to swim right out to sea. And finally, after millions of years, they were quite at home there.

Two of their descendants, the seal and the big tusked and whiskered walrus, are still born on land and frequently return there, to sit in friendly groups, or herds, basking in the sun. Both of these animals still have four stubby flippers that they use as feet.

But the rest of the seagoing mammals finally began to spend their whole lives in the water. Their hind legs became useless, hidden inside their skin so that they seem to have disappeared entirely. They developed tails which propel them forward. And they balance themselves, as fish do, with the fins or flippers that evolved from their forelegs. They almost completely lost their fur, although sometimes they have a few bristles here and there. A heavy layer of fat, or blubber, now takes the place of that warm coat. They lost the outer ear which mammals were the first to develop, and which is usually an outstanding characteristic of the whole class. In other words they came to look and behave very much like fish. But to this day they are still warm-blooded, and they still give birth to live young and nurse them.

The creatures that we now call porpoises and dolphins —sleek and playful animals that leap out of the water and slide back into it again with such marvelous grace—never

Whale

did grow very large. But their relatives, the whales, evolved into the largest mammals the world has ever known. Some of them are even larger than the biggest members of the reptile group, the gigantic dinosaurs. Whales have been known to grow to a length of more than a hundred feet and to a weight of almost a hundred tons.

Whales' teeth have developed in strange ways. Some whales kept much the same sort of teeth their land ancestors had, but others lost all except a few. The narwhal, for example, one member of the family, now has only two teeth. One of these remains hidden inside his skull. The other grows straight out from the front of his snout, twisted into a spiral-patterned stick that looks like an enormous tusk several feet long.

Some whales lost their teeth entirely, and acquired instead huge horny plates that hang down from the roof of their mouths. These plates, usually called whalebone, are sometimes six feet long. Along their edges are fringes which the whale uses for straining shrimps and even tinier animals and plants from the sea water he sucks into his mouth. This enormous creature manages to keep alive by eating some of the smallest kind of food available in the whole sea: plankton.

It is usually difficult to remember that whales are mammals, as are horses and dogs and men. But every time a whale "blows"—every time he exhales a great gust of warm air that turns to a column of steam rising above the water—he reminds us that his breathing apparatus is like our own. Unlike the fish among which he moves, he cannot breathe under water. He must come to the surface in order to inhale air, just as all mammals do. But he is indeed a dramatic indication of the great variety of forms into which the first tiny mammals evolved—a variety that was already very apparent by the end of the Eocene epoch.

13 *the golden age of mammals*

IT IS OFTEN DIFFICULT TO UNDERSTAND THE ENORMOUS periods of time so often mentioned in the story of pre-historic animals. In our everyday life we are accustomed to think in terms of days or weeks, or months or years. We know how swiftly a week slips by, how long a month can seem when we are waiting for some special event to happen at its end, and how very long it takes for twelve whole months to make up a single year. But when we read about an animal that lived one million years ago, or ten million years ago, or a hundred million years ago, those figures blur in our minds. They all sound almost alike because we cannot really imagine any of them.

Probably nobody can help us comprehend the actual length of time that is meant by "ten million years" or by "a hundred million years," but scientists have worked out a sort of calendar for helping us to understand the comparative lengths of the various periods in the history of prehistoric animals.

This calendar reduces three thousand million years of the earth's history to a single year, in much the same way that you can reduce the whole United States to a small map no larger than this page. Of course such a map does not show any details. It is not useful for locating your own house or your own street. But it does help you to understand where your town is located in your state and where your state is located in the nation. The scientists' big calendar is helpful in the same sort of way.

Each hundred years of time, on that calendar, is reduced to a single second. Sixty seconds, or one minute, represent 6,000 years. One hour represents 360,000 years, and one day represents about 8,640,000 years. Our own present time—the century we are now living in—is represented by the final second of the last minute just before midnight on December 31, the last day of that giant year. On this calendar, 134 "days" went by before there was any life on the earth at all, and another 75 "days" went by before the Cambrian period began and the trilobites became so numerous. In other words, assuming the year to start in January, the Cambrian period began on October 29, when this great "year" was already three quarters over. This means that all the rest of the story of prehistoric animals is squeezed into the few remaining months, with the Age of Reptiles beginning during the second week of December.

Mammals are very late arrivals among the animals of the earth. They did not become really important until December 26, when the "year" was nearly gone. And in the scant "week" that was left they changed and evolved into almost all the animals we know best in our world today.

The Eocene epoch, described in the last chapter, really lasted for about nineteen million years, but it represents only the first two "days" of that week. The next three epochs—the ten-million-year Oligocene, the twenty-million-year Miocene and the eight-million-year Pliocene—represent, all together, nearly four more days, and bring the calendar right up to December 31, the last day of this giant "year."

Those three epochs, therefore, cover a great deal of development, and at a very rapid rate. And we can understand that development only if we know what was happening to the earth itself during those three epochs, beginning about forty million years ago and ending only about one million years before our own day.

It was a time of striking change. In the beginning the climate was warm and moist, as it had been in the previous Eocene epoch. But gradually the climate cooled, and it continued to cool slowly but steadily throughout those many millions of years. Enormous mountain ranges were born—the towering Alps in Europe and the even higher Himalayas in Asia. Volcanoes were thrust up in many different parts of the world. All over the earth there was a gradual lifting of land and a related gradual decline in the level of the oceans.

Tender plants and tropical trees that needed warmth and moisture died out completely in many areas as these events took place. And slowly there began to appear the tough grasses that were the ancestors of all our modern grains. As time went by, those grasses spread farther and farther over the great cool high plains, until the plains finally became the vast meadows or grazing areas that today occupy thousands of square miles on almost every continent.

These striking changes of geography, of climate, and of plant life naturally brought about the extinction of the animals which proved unfit to survive in the new conditions. Certain mammals, for example, had teeth which had been perfectly suited to the kind of food they had always eaten in the past. The hard enamel coating of those teeth was very thin, but these short-crowned teeth, as scientists call them, did not wear away so long as the animals were chewing nothing but leaves and tender shoots. When the animals tried to eat the tough new grasses, however, the thin enamel wore away almost immediately and the unprotected teeth wore away too. Probably many animals died of starvation and whole races became extinct for this reason alone.

But other mammals developed new kinds of teeth, very well protected by enamel. These high-crowned teeth, as they are called, permitted the animals to eat even the toughest grasses without destroying their teeth, and therefore permitted them to survive. They became the world's first real grazing animals, ancestors of all the sheep, cows, horses, and other grass eaters of our present day. Herds of these grazing animals developed so rapidly and dramatically during the Miocene epoch that it has come to be known as the Golden Age of Mammals.

Among the many animals that flourished only for a time during the almost forty million years of those three ep-

Brontops

ochs, and that became extinct before the end of the last one, were many varieties of both plant eaters and meat eaters. In most cases they belonged to families or groups that had been numerous and important in an earlier period.

The family of titanotheres, for example, which had been represented by little *Palaeosyops* during the Eocene epoch, produced in the Oligocene big *Brontops*, whose name means "thunder head." This ponderous, hoofed plant eater grew to a length of fourteen feet and stood six feet high at the shoulder. He carried his great weight on thick elephantlike legs that ended in wide circular feet, and his saddle-shaped head looked rather like the head of a modern rhinoceros. He had blunt hornlike growths on the front of that head, and scientists think one *Brontops* sometimes attacked another with those weapons.

Archaeotherium

Brontops skeletons have been found with ribs that had been broken and healed again before the animals' death. Scientists believe that only another *Brontops* could have inflicted rib-breaking blows on these big beasts.

But in spite of his power and size, *Brontops* survived for only a comparatively short period. One reason for his extinction at the end of the Oligocene epoch may have been that his brain was very small. Then, too, his low-crowned teeth may have been unable to adapt to the new food supply, the harder grasses that were becoming plentiful.

Although not so large as *Brontops*, another powerful plant eater of the same period was *Archeotherium*. He was not a pig, but he looked so much like one that he is often called a "giant pig." His remarkably long head was equipped with a pair of rounded bone plates extending sideways just below his eyes, and with four bone knobs on his lower jaw. A later, Miocene member of this long-headed, piglike family was *Dinohyus*, six feet high at the shoulder, and with bony projections on his upper jaw and teeth so thick and strong that they were probably useful as weapons.

A very different sort of animal was graceful little *Protoceras*, about the size of a pointer dog. Its gazellelike body was supported by long slender legs, and the female was probably a very charming creature. But the male wore two short strong tusks and a grotesque assortment of blunt hornlike growths, one pair over his eyes, one above his mouth, and one on the back of his head. He lived in the Oligocene epoch and soon became extinct, but he had relatives in each of the two following epochs. One of them, *Syndyoceras*, which lived in the Miocene, was about as large as a deer and nearly as graceful. The rear pair of his bony growths were curved like a cow's horns, and the front pair were joined at the base and flared outward in

Protoceras

Synthetoceras

the shape of a *V*. A still later member of this same family,
Synthetoceras, also had a graceful body and strange horny
growths on his head. One pair rose up behind his eyes, and
a third projection jutted up above his nostrils, dividing
into two branches to form a *Y*.

A large group of animals that were particularly numerous in North America during the Oligocene and Miocene epochs were the oreodonts. Certain members of the
group remained in the forests; others seemed to become
well adapted to the grassy plains that were covering more
and more of the earth; and still others apparently stayed
so close to the water that scientists think they may have
been as aquatic as the modern water-loving hippopota-

mus. Fossil remains of these creatures are quite common and numbers of them are often found close together, because oreodonts tended to travel in herds or groups. Scientists searching eagerly for clues to some rarer animals sometimes find such an abundance of oreodont fossils that they begin to think of them as a nuisance.

One of the early and most abundant members of this family was *Merycoidodon*, which had a rather calflike head and a rather piglike body about four feet long. The first part of his name comes from the Greek word *meryx*, which means "ruminating animal." A form of that Greek word appearing in a prehistoric animal's name indicates that the scientist who named the animal believed it ruminated, or chewed a cud.

A later and slightly larger member of the same group was *Merycochoerus*, which had a heavy boarlike body, a long head, and a sizable snout. He probably spent a great deal of time in the water, eating the soft plants and roots for which his teeth were well adapted. But one of his smaller, more slender relatives, *Merychyus*, developed real

Merycochoerus

grazing teeth with high crowns—the kind of teeth all modern ruminants, or cud chewers, have. These teeth continued to grow steadily throughout the animal's life. A diet of tough grass caused them to wear away slowly on top, but continual growth kept them at the same height year after year.

Two other plant eaters that flourished for a time during the Miocene epoch, while the oreodonts were still numerous, were *Moropus* and *Merycodus*.

Moropus

Merycodus

Moropus belonged to the chalicotheres, a family distinguished by its cleft toes with stout claws. He was a curious animal that would probably have looked to us, at first glance, rather like a large, very badly constructed horse. His head, at any rate, was very much like a horse's head, but it was small in comparison to his big body. And the head was lifted high into the air, because his forelegs were longer than his hind legs and his back slanted sharply upward from low hips. His thick, heavy legs were also very different from the slender hoofed legs of a horse. Scientists are not sure whether he used his big claws as weapons of defense or for tearing roots and plants out of the ground. But those big clawed feet certainly helped to emphasize the awkwardness of his ungainly body.

Merycodus, on the other hand, was an extremely grace-

Hoplophoneus

ful creature about the size of a small deer, with a slim short-tailed body and branching horns. Some scientists think he may have been an ancestor of modern deer, although others think he was probably an ancestor of the modern pronghorn, which now lives in the western United States and Mexico.

All of these plant eaters naturally had meat-eating enemies, and some of those meat eaters became extinct, too, as time went by. But whether they became extinct or not, a surprising number of them bore at least a slight resemblance to certain animals in our modern world.

Hyaenodon, for example, a survivor of the ancient creodont group, rather resembled the present-day animal for which he has been named, the hyena. *Hyaenodon* was often heavily built; scientists have found skulls as large as those of grizzly bears. This animal may have been able to stalk and kill some of the larger hoofed mammals of its time.

Hyaenodon's neighbor, catlike *Hoplophoneus*, was certainly a real hunter, and must have been a very dangerous enemy. He was sometimes as big as a mountain lion, with enormously powerful muscles. His two huge upper canine teeth were actually long tusks that came far down over his lower jaw. And his lower jaw had bony extensions, or guards, against which the teeth rested when the animal's mouth was closed. He must have had to open his jaw very wide indeed, and strike downward with his whole head, in order to stab at his prey with those daggerlike teeth.

A later meat eater similarly equipped with great saber-like teeth was *Thylacosmilus*, which lived in South America. But the curious thing about this definitely catlike creature was that he had no relation to the cat family at all. He was actually a marsupial—a member of the group to which the kangaroo belongs.

Some other meat eaters of this time are confusing in that they resembled one group of modern animals while they may have been the ancestors of other quite different groups.

Big-headed, long-tailed, short-legged *Daphoenus*, for example, probably looked rather like a modern dog. But scientists think he may have been a remote ancestor of

Amphicyon

the so-called bear-dogs, which may in turn have been remote ancestors of the now extinct short-faced bears. Later doglike animals such as *Amphicyon* and *Dinocyon*, were almost as large as grizzly bears and perhaps even more deadly, because they were so much faster on their feet than modern bears are.

Cynodictis, which had a weasel-like appearance, was probably the true although very remote ancestor of modern dogs. This seems particularly surprising because this rather small slender creature which lived in Europe about forty million years ago had claws which he could extend or pull back. And claws of this type, called retractile claws, are usually regarded in the present day as characteristic of cats. Nevertheless *Cynodictis* seems to have been an ancestor of little doglike *Tomarctus*, which appeared in the Miocene epoch and was almost certainly the predecessor of all modern dogs and wolves.

During the three epochs, Oligocene, Miocene, and Pliocene, when the grasses were spreading over the earth and so many different kinds of mammals were developing —some to become extinct, others to carry their races forward toward the present—great strides were made by those four important mammal families, the rhinoceroses, the elephants, the camels, and the horses.

During the first of the three epochs there were many representatives of the rhinoceroses, and they lived in almost all parts of the world except Australia and South America. They ranged in size from slender-legged, quick little *Hyracodon*, which was probably no bigger than a pony, to the huge hornless monster called *Baluchitherium*, which stood seventeen feet high at the shoulders. This

Baluchitherium

great lumbering plant eater was probably the biggest land mammal that ever lived. He dwarfed even that giant meat-eating mammal of an earlier period, bloodthirsty *Andrewsarchus*, whose skull was a yard long. *Baluchitherium* would probably have looked quite at home, as far as size was concerned, in the time of the gigantic dinosaurs.

When he became extinct, this huge animal did not leave any direct descendants. Scientists believe that a much smaller mammal, *Trigonias*, was the true ancestor of the rhinoceroses that live today in Africa and parts of Asia. *Trigonias* had heavy legs and big feet, and his head had the characteristic saddle shape of modern members of

Diceratherium

the family. But he had no horns. Later members of the family, however, did acquire this characteristic of the modern rhinoceros. *Diceratherium*, for example, had heavy legs and a heavy body about the size of a wild boar with two horns side by side on the tip of his nose. And his larger relative, *Teleoceras*—which had the typical saddle-shaped head of the modern rhinoceros, and the modern animal's three-toed feet—had a horn on the tip of his nose.

It is not always easy for scientists to tell whether or not a prehistoric rhinoceros had horns, because rhinoceros horns do not make good fossils. They are not composed partly or wholly of bone, like the so-called "horns" of all other animals. They consist entirely of real horn, which —like hoofs and claws, and like the scales of fish and the feathers of birds—is really a specialized version of skin, or what scientists call "modified skin." Horn, in other words, is really a mass of tough fibers held together by a kind of natural glue. And this substance usually disintegrates after a time and leaves no fossil remains at all. But sometimes the nose bones of a prehistoric rhinoceros skeleton have rough knobby spots at certain points, and scientists think these spots show where horns once grew. When they found such a spot on a skeleton of *Teleoceras*, for example, they were quite sure that member of the family had a horn.

The elephant family, in the meantime, was also developing noticeably toward its long-trunked modern representatives. Two important early African members of the group, for example, *Phiomia* and *Paleomastodon*, were both considerably smaller than modern elephants, but they had already acquired short trunks and tusks. *Phiomia* probably evolved into the later four-tusked *Trilophodon*, whose bulky body stood about five feet high and whose lower jaw thrust forward almost as far as his trunk did. This particular branch of the family apparently be-

Teleoceras

came extinct eventually, but not before one variety had developed lower tusks so broad they could be used as shovels.

The other branch, however, descending from *Paleomastodon*, or "ancient mastodon," evolved into large *Pliomastodon*, or "more like a mastodon." And with *Pliomastodon* the signs of the modern elephant were becoming very clear. He had a real trunk, and the tusks growing out of his upper jaw curved upward, just as the tusks of modern elephants do.

Alticamelus

While this growth and change was going on, the various members of the elephant family, or Proboscidea, as scientists call them, were engaged in a forty-million-year journey that during its course took them from their original home in Africa to almost every other part of the world. They wandered eastward across Asia, crossed the land bridge then connecting Asia with Alaska, and spread southward and westward throughout the Western Hemisphere. For a time they were a common sight on the great plains of the American Midwest. Certainly they have been among the most traveled families in mammal history.

The camel family followed somewhat the same pattern that the elephants did. They produced some branches that eventually became extinct, but through other branches they evolved slowly toward the characteristically humped creatures of today.

One early member of the family, sheep-sized *Poebrotherium*, really looked very much like the South American llama, a modern relative of the camel. He had slender legs like a llama's, with the hind legs longer than the forelegs. His originally low-crowned teeth were developing higher crowns, so that he was adapting himself to the eating of tough grass. And he had already acquired one marked characteristic of the modern camel: the two-toed foot.

As time went by, some members of the family remained fairly small and gazellelike, and others grew large. *Alticamelus*, or "tall camel," was one of the giants of the group. He had an extremely long neck, and long spindly legs all of the same size, so that his back was straight. Probably he also had some sort of spongy elastic pads

Megacamelus

on his feet, like the ones modern camels have, but he probably had no hump. He finally became extinct.

It is probably his relative, *Procamelus*, or "early camel," that deserves the name of father to the whole camel-llama tribe. He too looked quite like a llama, with a long, gently curved neck and a long head on his sheep-sized body. His two-toed feet were equipped with soft pads on which he could probably move tirelessly over the plains, grazing the rich new grass crop. One of his descendants, much larger than himself—taller, in fact, than a modern elephant—was fifteen-foot-high *Megacamelus*, or "big camel." Perhaps this creature was the first of the camel family to wear a hump; he may have had at least a small one over his shoulders.

The evolution of the camel is likely to be confusing to a layman, but that of the horse is less difficult to follow. Even the very earliest horse looked quite horselike, although he was extremely small. And during the millions of years that followed, the various descendants of that little animal grew steadily larger and more like the horse of today.

During the early part of the forty-million-year span we are now considering, *Mesohippus,* descendant of earlier eohippus, reached the size of a greyhound. His legs were long and slender, and his back was straighter than the arched back of eohippus, or "dawn horse." He still had low-crowned teeth, and undoubtedly browsed on leaves and soft shoots rather than on grass. But his feet were evolving toward the feet of today's horses. He had three toes on each foot, with the large center toe carrying most of the weight. In still later members of the family those central toes would grow larger still, and the others would shrink until finally the horse was walking entirely on the single large central toe that carries his hoof today.

That development was already taking place during the Pliocene epoch. *Pliohippus,* one of the horses of that time, was not yet as large as a modern horse, but already he walked on a single toe. The other two toes on each foot were so small that they could be seen only in the animal's skeleton; they did not form actual toes visible through the skin. *Pliohippus* was also beginning to have real grazing teeth, small in size as yet, but probably capable of chewing grass with some efficiency. Another member of the family which appeared before the Pliocene epoch ended truly deserved his name, *Plesippus,* which means "almost horse." He was larger than his forefathers, and his legs were sturdier than the earlier horses' legs, although they were still slender. His teeth were fully capable of

Epigaulus

withstanding a steady diet of harsh grass. They were high-crowned, and they grew continually, replacing the grinding surface that wore away constantly during his lifetime. In every way *Plesippus* was indeed "almost horse."

By the end of those almost forty million years—by the time the Oligocene, the Miocene, and the Pliocene epochs had come to a close—the rhinoceroses, the elephants, the camels, and the horses would all have been more or less recognizable, even to nonexperts, as ancestors of the animals we know today. By that time, too, other families of animals had made similar advances. The little rodents, for example, were multiplying rapidly and evolving into many new types. One curious member of the family was the horned gopher, *Epigaulus*, which was probably much larger than the modern rodent, and had, rising between his eyes, two hornlike projections such as no modern rodent possesses. But at about the same time other gophers developed that were ancestors of modern animals. Along with them there evolved primitive rats, mice, beavers, squirrels,

and rabbits. And somehow, in spite of the fact that the
world had become crowded with hungry big mammals,
these little creatures managed to survive and leave descendants to our modern world.

One broiling hot day in the year 1948 a group of paleontologists was exploring the gulleys and ancient lake
beds of a small island near the edge of Lake Victoria, in
East Africa. The sun glared down on the whitish earth
and the heat was almost unbearable. But they stuck to
their back-breaking job, crawling painfully over the
ground on a search that had already lasted for years.

Thousands of fossils lay scattered over the area—so
many bones and fragments of bones that the parched
ground looked like a pebbled beach. All the fossils dated
from the Miocene epoch and were perhaps twelve or
fifteen million years old. But most of them won only a
glance or two before they were discarded. They were
crocodile vertebrae and bits of tortoise shell, fossils so
common in that neighborhood that the scientists were no
longer interested in collecting them. Sometimes one of
the men did pick up a bone and study it under a magnify-
ing glass, because millions of years ago a *Hyaenodon* had
gnawed it to shapelessness and the scientist could not be
certain what it was. But one by one the most hopeful-
looking specimens were laid aside. None of them had
proved to be the one particular bone the scientists were
seeking—a bone no paleontologist had yet found anywhere in the world.

Then suddenly the wife of the expedition leader, Dr.
L. S. B. Leakey, called out to her husband. A moment

later the whole group had gathered around her, scarcely daring to believe their eyes. Mrs. Leakey had actually discovered the very prize they had all dreamed of finding. Before her on the ground lay the nearly perfect skull of an ape that had lived millions of years ago in the Miocene epoch.

Not many days later Dr. and Mrs. Leakey set out by plane for London, to show the precious skull to other experts and to have it studied and tested. The prehistoric bone had been insured for thousands of dollars, but Mrs. Leakey insisted upon carrying it carefully in her lap for the entire journey. And she breathed a great sigh of relief when she delivered it safely to its destination. It had been worth all the long years of patient and difficult search. It was the most ancient nearly complete ape skull ever found anywhere.

Apes, of course, belong to the group of mammals called primates, of which little lemurlike *Notharctus* was an Eocene example. During the Oligocene epoch other types had appeared, like *Propliopithecus*, the first-known real ape. Scientists still don't know a great deal about this little creature that probably lived high in the trees of the ancient forests. But they do know that his jaws were quite small, and that his tooth pattern was like the tooth pattern of a human being. And they think he may have been the ancestor of all modern apes and of that other branch of the primate family—human beings.

Apes and monkeys apparently became quite common during the Miocene and Pliocene epochs, and many fossils of such creatures had turned up before Mrs. Leakey made her important discovery of the first nearly complete Miocene ape skull. Probably those prehistoric creatures were completely or almost completely covered with hair, as most such animals are today. Many of them had lengthy tails. They probably walked on all fours, as most other land mammals did, but some of them could probably walk on their hind legs alone. This meant that they could use their forelegs as arms for swinging through the trees, and their fingers for grasping.

The development of the primates was perhaps the most exciting event in that whole forty-million-year span, so far as we are concerned. And of course it would be even more exciting if some day a searcher discovered the unmistakable fossil remains of a man that lived before the end of that long period. At present, however, paleontologists think that such a discovery is unlikely.

The evolutionary process had produced a great and wide variety of mammals before the end of the Pliocene epoch about a million years ago. But it did not, apparently, produce a human being until the next and last of the many epochs of the earth's prehistoric life: the age of ice and mammoths and man, known as the Pleistocene or "most recent."

14 *the drama of the Ice Age*

SOME PEOPLE SPEAK OF THE ICE AGE AS IF IT WERE A
period long ago when the whole world was covered with
ice. There never was such a time, so far as scientists know.
It is true, however, that on four separate occasions during
the Pleistocene epoch, which began about a million years
ago, enormous sheets of ice did cover great areas of the
Northern Hemisphere. Each of those separate ice ages,
or glacial periods as they are called, lasted for thousands
of years. But the thousands of years between one and
another were periods of fairly mild climate, sometimes
even milder than the climate of the world today.

The first big ice sheets probably began to form, very
slowly, many thousands of years after the start of the
Pleistocene epoch. The weather had turned much colder
by then, and it remained cold over a long period. Small
patches of ice around the North Pole grew thicker and
thicker as the temperature dropped; they finally spread
out to form vast sheets of ice, glaciers more than a mile

thick in some places and stretching almost all the way around the globe. They actually flowed southward too, pushing tons of huge boulders and stones ahead of them as they moved. And they continued to grow and spread until they covered much of northern Europe, almost all of Canada, and parts of the United States.

Then the climate changed and the weather began to grow warmer again. The southernmost edges of the ice melted and the sheets of ice shrank, leaving enormous ridges of piled rock and debris where their outer boundaries had been. Scientists say the glaciers were "retreating." After thousands of years they were reduced again to small polar icecaps, and almost the whole earth blossomed in the gentle new warmth. Before the climate changed once more, and the second ice sheets began to form, tropical plants could grow in lands that today support only hardy trees and bushes.

But long before the first ice sheet spread and retreated, the animals of the world had taken part in a strange mass migration—a vast slow expansion of their range—that carried them from continent to continent and enormously affected their development.

That great movement apparently began early in the Pleistocene epoch, or possibly even just before that period began. The weather was already growing colder then, and the small polar icecaps—not yet ready to spread southward—were thickening rapidly. This thickening process absorbed much of the seas' water, and all over the earth the level of the oceans sank. Continent-connecting land bridges, flooded for many centuries, were once more exposed. And when those bridges—between Siberia and

Alaska, and between North and South America—became passable, the mammals of the world began to travel across them. For thousands of years, for thousands of generations, great herds of animals spread farther and farther from the regions where they had long made their homes.

Animals from the Old World moved into the North American continent and animals of the Western Hemisphere journeyed into Asia and on into Europe. South American animals traveled northward into what is now the United States, and North American animals traveled southward across the Isthmus of Panama.

Scientists do not know why this mass migration took place. They only know that it did happen and that during the course of those lengthy journeys the process of evolution speeded up. Many animals of the world became extinct, while others—adapting rapidly to the changing conditions of their lives—evolved into modern or almost modern forms.

The one part of the world completely unaffected by these mass movements was the great island continent of Australia. Then, as now, it was cut off from the rest of the world by long miles of ocean. The animals that had already lived there for millions of years remained there in isolation. From that time until the present they evolved in their own special direction. And for this reason the modern Australian kangaroo is very unlike its distant marsupial relatives in other lands, and the modern Australian platypus has no living relatives anywhere at all.

Scientists have been able to trace quite clearly the journeys taken by certain families of mammals. They know a good deal about the movements of four important groups: camels, horses, rhinoceroses, and elephants; and the ways in which those animals changed as they wandered.

For example, some members of the camel family, which had long made their home in North America, crossed into South America, where they evolved into the llamas and alpacas that inhabit the mountains of that continent today. Other larger camels crossed into Asia to become the ancestors of present-day Asiatic and African members of the tribe.

North American horses, in the meantime, were spreading throughout almost the entire world. For most of the Pleistocene epoch they inhabited every continent except Australia. And by that time the horse family had at last produced the animal that has been called *Equus*. This name simply means "horse," and *Equus* is the modern horse.

Although his development can be traced quite accurately, scientists still cannot solve one mystery in the life of the horse family. They do not know why all horses suddenly disappeared from the whole Western Hemisphere at some time toward the end of the Pleistocene epoch. While horses continued to flourish in Europe and Asia and Africa, the continents of North and South America were without any horses at all for thousands of years. Horses reappeared in the New World only when explorers from Europe brought them, a few centuries ago.

The members of the rhinoceros family, which we think of today as inhabiting only the warmer parts of the world, developed heavy coats of fur during the Pleistocene epoch and were apparently able to live quite close to the big ice sheets. Apparently none of them ever found their way into the Western Hemisphere, but they did travel widely over Europe and Asia. Some of these animals, remarkably well preserved, have been found buried in the frozen earth of Siberia. And one complete fossil rhinoceros was dug up in a part of Poland where the soil oozes petroleum. The oil had "pickled" the body and prevented it from decaying. These valuable fossil discoveries prove to us that the rhinoceros of that period wore two horns much like his descendants today, but he looked quite different from a modern rhinoceros because of his woolly coat. It consisted of an underlayer of short fine fur, and an over-layer of longer, coarser hair.

Warm coats of very much the same kind were also developed by the elephant family, which flourished so astonishingly during the Pleistocene epoch that it was probably the most important and outstanding mammal group in many parts of the world at that time. The tusks worn by those long-dead animals, and collected by modern Siberian ivory hunters, have supplied the present-day world with about half its total supply of ivory.

Great herds of hairy mastodons, survivals of the previous period, ranged the forested hills of the New World from Alaska to Mexico. They still had the low-crowned teeth of their ancestors, and probably lived chiefly on leaves, but they looked very much like modern elephants. And they must have been very adaptable animals because they survived until perhaps fifteen or twenty thousand years ago.

In the meantime some of their newer relatives were also becoming important. All the members of this newer group are scientifically classified as true elephants, al-

Mastodon

though they are better known as mammoths. Old World mammoths crossed the Bering Strait bridge during the time of the mass migration, and spread widely throughout North America.

All mammoths had trunks and tusks. The trunks were undoubtedly useful for grasping the high-growing leaves of trees, and in many cases the tusks probably served as weapons and also for rooting up plants. But some of those tusks are very puzzling to a modern scientist, because they curved in such a way that their tips crossed each other, and it is difficult to imagine how an animal could have used them for either digging or fighting.

But scientists do not question the efficiency of the mammoths' teeth, all of which were very like the teeth of the present-day elephant. In fact, those teeth were probably the most efficient grinding machines any plant-eater ever developed. A mammoth had several large grinding teeth in each jaw, but he chewed with only four of them—two in the upper jaw and two in the lower. The others, just behind them, were what we might call spare teeth. When, in spite of their heavy layer of hard enamel, the four working grinders finally wore down to stubs, the spare teeth behind them began to move forward along the jaw until the worn teeth were finally pushed out and the new ones could take their place. This system provided the mammoths with good grinding equipment throughout their lives.

Among the several varieties of mammoths roaming the earth during the Pleistocene epoch were the plains-loving imperial mammoth, over thirteen feet tall and with immense tusks thirteen or more feet long, and the smaller woolly mammoths whose double-layered fur coats were so warm that these animals could live in the far north close to the edge of the ice. Their outer layer of coarse brown hair sometimes grew to a length of twenty inches, and a heavy layer of fat beneath their thick skin gave them further protection against the cold. We know a great deal about these mammoths because several complete animals —not simply their skeletons, but their flesh and hairy hide as well—have been discovered in the perpetually frozen

Woolly mammoth

earth of Siberia, where the fine woolly rhinoceros fossils were also found.

Modern elephants undoubtedly first evolved in the Old World and apparently never wandered over into the Western Hemisphere along with their mammoth relatives. Modern elephants are still found only in Asia and Africa, in the same warm lands that were probably their homes long ago. These great lumbering beasts, with their long trunks and their handsome tusks, are not quite so large as some of their ancestors, and certainly not so numerous. But they are the only members of the family that survived up to the present day, and they are the largest land animals inhabiting our modern world.

As the great sheets of ice slowly advanced over tremendous areas of Europe and North America, thousands and thousands of animals were driven southward in their struggle for survival. In North America, for example, as

Irish elk

the first sheet of ice advanced as far south as Nebraska, the inhabitants of Canada were forced into what is now the United States, where they had to compete for food with all the animals already making their home there. This kind of competition hastened the development of some groups and the extinction of others—the extinction of those not strong enough to fight for food, and those not able to adapt to new diets and new conditions.

The short-faced bears, some of them large and very powerful, were among the animals that became extinct during the ebb and flow of the ice sheets. But the true bears, whose ancestry is still not entirely clear, were successfully evolving throughout the Ice Age. Some of them journeyed from their home in the Old World into North America, where they have survived to this day.

Other animals were evolving toward modern deer, antelopes, oxen, sheep, and goats. Some of the Ice Age deer were truly enormous. The giant Irish elk had nine-foot antlers which sometimes weighed more than the animal's entire skeleton. But musk oxen and bison, now almost entirely extinct, were probably the two most important members of the group at that time. Great herds of them wandered across Europe and Asia and into North America. Bison populated our own continent as far south as Florida and Mexico.

Both musk oxen and bison were well protected against

Musk ox

Felis atrox

the bitter cold of the Ice Age. The bison of that period, which stood six feet high and wore great horns that measured six feet from tip to tip, had long shaggy fur over his huge shoulder hump and short woolly fur over his hind quarters. The short-legged, heavily built musk oxen, whose horns sometimes joined at the base to form a kind of tough helmet, and curved forward at the tips to serve as menacing weapons, had a double fur coat like that of a woolly mammoth.

Today there are only a few herds of musk oxen still alive in Greenland, in the cold barren waste of northern Canada, and in Vermont, where they have recently been introduced as an agricultural experiment. Although there were thousands of bison—or buffalo, as they are usually called—still roaming the plains when the first white settlers came to North America, almost all of them were destroyed by the white hunters. There would be none at all left today if the governments of Canada and the United

States had not passed laws to protect the last few that escaped the hunters' greed.

The cat family and the dog family were also important during the Ice Age, and in general those meat eaters were larger and fiercer than their descendants of today.

One of the cats of that period was *Felis atrox*, an ancestor of the modern lion. He looked very much like his descendant, except that he was considerably larger and had no mane. Like a modern lion, he was probably a swift and successful hunter. Saber-toothed *Smilodon*, often incorrectly called a saber-toothed tiger, had distinctly catlike features. Because he was short-legged and not a very good runner, he probably lay in wait for his victims at a water hole, where he seized them and stabbed them to death with his long scimitarlike teeth.

The big Ice Age members of the dog family were probably equally dangerous to the plant eaters of their day. One of them, the six-foot-long dire wolf, sometimes ate

Smilodon

Dire wolf

carrion, but he also sometimes traveled in packs on the hunt for live prey, running a victim until it was exhausted and then closing in for the kill.

But two of the largest animals of the period were less dangerous than they must have appeared to their neighbors, because one was a herbivore and the other probably lived chiefly on carrion.

The carrion eater, a native of South America and apparently related to the modern armadillo, was called *Glyptodon*. A heavy-domed armor protected his whole body, which sometimes stood five feet high and measured fourteen feet from head to tip of tail. The tail was armored too, and might end in a cluster of sharp spikes as deadly as an ancient war club. If an enemy approached, *Glyptodon* could squat low on the ground so that his armor formed an igloolike shell over his whole body, leaving only the tail exposed to flail at any animal that dared to get within his range.

The largest of the many giant animals of the whole Pleistocene epoch, the herbivore called *Megatherium*, was a native of South America and the Southeastern United States. He was a ground sloth, a distant relative of the curious modern sloth family, one member of which habitually hangs upside down from a tree limb. *Megatherium* was larger than a modern elephant and looked rather like a huge bear. From the tip of his long narrow head to the tip of his massive tail he sometimes measured twenty feet. The one powerful curved claw on each of his hind feet, and the three hooked claws on each front foot may have been very useful for digging up roots or for fending off the attack of a ferocious carnivore. Scientists believe *Megatherium* often stood on his hind legs, propping himself in place with his tail, and using his clawed forefeet to pull high branches down within reach. He probably had a long flexible tongue too, which helped him to pull

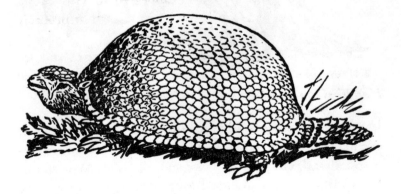

Glyptodon

Megatherium

leaves into his mouth. Like many members of the ancient edentate or "toothless" family, to which both *Megatherium* and *Glyptodon* belonged, he did have simple teeth that were several inches long.

Megatherium's legs were short, and he could waddle

only slowly and awkwardly, putting all his weight on the outer edges of his turned-under feet. But in spite of this handicap the members of his family did wander up into what is now the United States. Their fossil remains have been found as far north as New Jersey.

It is not surprising, of course, that the scientific detectives of our own day have been able to learn a great deal about the animals that lived in the Pleistocene epoch. That time is comparatively close to our own, and fossils from it are particularly abundant. Paleontologists have been able to find and study the skeletons of all the creatures mentioned in this chapter, and of such other Ice Age animals as foxes, coyotes, pumalike cats, raccoons, weasels, otters, tapirs, the wild pigs called peccaries, and all sorts of rodents, including a giant beaver the size of a small bear.

In a single place in Los Angeles, for example, searchers have found enormous numbers of Ice Age fossils preserved in huge tar pits. Those La Brea tar pits, as they are called, existed during the Ice Age as they do today, and served as a natural trap for unwary animals. Every trapped animal attracted hungry carnivores or carrion eaters, who gathered around to feast on the victim—and they themselves were often trapped as they fought over the carcass. Even carrion-eating *Teratornis*, a relative of the modern condor, was caught in the adhesive tar of the pits. That giant vulture had a wing spread of twelve feet and was one of the largest flying birds that ever lived.

But in spite of all we know of the Pleistocene animals, one great event of that period is still wrapped in mystery. Scientists have no explanation for the fact that after the

Teratornis

last icecap started to retreat, all the largest and strongest Ice Age animals began to die out in the temperate zones of the world—in the very places where they had apparently enjoyed the most favorable climate and living conditions. They did not all die out in Africa, or in certain parts of Asia, where to this day there are elephants, rhinoceroses, and other large representatives of ancient animal groups. But on three fifths of the earth, in all of North and South America, and in the temperate zones of

Europe and Asia, the largest members of each family vanished, and in some cases a family vanished entirely. The mammoths and the mastodons, for example, had become extinct in those areas soon after the close of the Pleistocene epoch, which ended about twenty thousand years ago. By that same time, in those temperate zones, the largest cats, dogs, sloths, deer, oxen, and bison had also disappeared. Today only smaller members of those groups survive in that part of the world.

The sudden disappearance of those giants, after they had successfully endured the rigors of the Ice Age, is as mysterious as the swift extinction of the giant dinosaurs a hundred million years earlier. Scientists searching for an explanation can only say, as they say of the dinosaurs, that their death probably did not result from any one single cause. Climatic change and competition for food may have helped to hasten their end. And a comparatively small creature may possibly have helped to bring about the extinction of the giant mammals after they had reached their greatest size and power. That small creature which may have helped to destroy those giant mammals was, of course, early man.

The story of early man is still largely a mystery. How he evolved from an ancient ancestor, from some primate that was probably the ancestor of certain manlike apes as well, is still not clear. Paleontologists have found some clues to the mystery, such as fossil bones of creatures that were probably not exactly like modern man but that were evolving toward modern man; and they have tried to arrange these clues in order.

There exists, for example, a part of a skeleton dug up

in China in 1928. It probably belonged to a creature that walked erect, and that had a fairly large brain. Near his bones were other charred bones, rude tools, and bits of charcoal, which tell us that this creature was probably a hunter and knew how to use fire. Because of his erect posture, big brain, and the evidence that he used tools and fire, we think this creature was probably a very early man. Scientists call him Peking Man, because his bones were found near the city of Peking, or Peiping. They believe he lived about four hundred thousand years ago, during the Ice Age.

To other bones that appear to be human or almost human, scientists have given other names, and have tried to date them by the newest chemical tests. They have come to believe, among other things, that a modern man probably did not exist until about fifty thousand years ago.

The story of man's evolution will not be complete until many more fossils have been found and studied. But scientists already know that even early man did not need his arms and hands to help him get about. He could use them instead for holding things and making things. And he probably had a better brain than any creature that had ever lived before him.

Because man had this good brain he evolved in the way he did. Other creatures had been able to kill only animals smaller or weaker than themselves. But, as he evolved over thousands of years, man's brain helped him to make tools and weapons with which he could kill even those animals that were larger and stronger than he was. By using his brain he slowly learned to plant crops to increase his food supply, and to make clothes and shelters that protected him from weather that might otherwise have caused his death. Of course his brain also enabled him eventually to construct a language, and to put it into written, or permanent, form. When he could write down the things he knew and descriptions of the world about him, he was able to preserve what he had learned for those who came after him. In this way each generation could know more than did the one before, and man could develop more rapidly than other creatures, which were able to learn only from their own experience.

Of course, when man could write down his thoughts and his knowledge, the prehistoric period was over. By that time—by the time he could write a history of his world—man had already become its ruler, and has remained its ruler ever since.

He lives largely now in a temperate climate, with weather that is growing slowly but steadily warmer. For the past twenty thousand years the fourth great icecap has been retreating, until nothing is left of it but areas of ice around the poles, and a few glaciers that still flow downward from the peaks of snow-tipped mountains. It seems likely, however, that the weather will turn cold again, after perhaps another fifty thousand years, and that a fifth glacial period will then begin.

Man's brain, which is able to study clues to the past and to the future, has made him a powerful earth ruler. Probably no other creature ever controlled the planet as completely as he does. His rule has lasted only a very short time, of course, compared to the long existence of the tiny trilobites, which endured for millions of years. No one knows how long man will continue to be dominant. He can use his brain to protect himself from all sorts of natural dangers of the kind that destroyed many animals in the past. But he has used his brain to invent weapons of destruction also—weapons that can destroy thousands of his own kind in a single great explosion.

A dinosaur presumably killed only one other dinosaur at a time, and then only when he was hungry. Man is far more intelligent than the dinosaur. He is clever enough to have collected and interpreted the clues that tell him the dinosaur's story. So perhaps man will prove intelligent enough not to use the weapons he has invented to bring about his own extinction. Then, perhaps, his rule of the earth may extend for countless years into the future. Man may even last as long as the tiny-brained dinosaurs or the little sea-dwelling trilobites.

other books to read

ANDREWS, ROY CHAPMAN All about dinosaurs. Random House, Inc., New York, 1953.

BAITY, ELIZABETH CHESLEY America before man. The Viking Press, Inc., New York, 1953.

COLBERT, EDWIN H. The dinosaur book. The American Museum of Natural History, New York, 1945.

FENTON, CARROLL LANE Life long ago; the story of fossils. John Day Company, Inc., New York, 1937.

SCHEELE, WILLIAM EARLE Prehistoric animals. The World Publishing Company, Cleveland, Ohio, 1954.

WHITE, ANNE TERRY Prehistoric America. Random House, Inc., New York, 1951.

index

mosasaurs, 107
of mountains, 4
multituberculates, 124
Oligocene epochs, 11
Ornithischia, 74
ostracoderm, 29
oviparous, 109
ovoviviparous, 108-109
Paleocene epoch, 11
Paleomastodon, 164
paleontologist, 2
of paleontology, 2
Paleozoic era, 10
periods, 10
of petrified, 2-3
Phobosuchus, 83
placoderms, 30
Plateosaurus. 75
Plesiadapis, 127
Plesippus, 167
Pleistocene epoch, 11
Pliocene epoch, 11
of *Pliomastodon,* 164
of *Procamelus,* 166
Proterozoic era, 10
protozoa, 39
Psittacosaurus, 98
pterosaur, 112
reptile, 61
Rhamphorhynchus, 112
of rhynchocephalians, 83
Saurischia, 74
sauros, 73
Seymouria, 59
Squamata, 85
strata, 6
Styracosaurus, 100
teleost, 33
theriodonts, 65
Titanichthys, 30
titanotheres, 133-134
Trachodon, 92
ungulates, 128
viviparous, 109
worm cast, 3

F

Felis atrox, 183

Fishes
and amphibians, 52
giant bulldog, 33
and great landward migration,
45-57
Higher Bony, 32-36
imitation
in Eocene epoch, 140-141
and ichthyosaur, 109
lobe-finned, 33-36
bladder evolution into lungs, 51
descendants of, 49-52
survival of, 50-52
lung, 34
marlin, 34
ray-finned, 33
sailfish, 34
shiner, 34
swordfish, 34
and swimming reptiles, 109-110
Fly, 47-48
Fossil
of *Archaeopteryx,* 116
of birds, 116
and bone, 2-3
brachiopods, 17-19
bryozoans, 20-21
of *Carcharodon megalodon,* 32
of clams, 21
as clues, 4
to history, 6-9, 13, 115
and identification of periods,
11
and life in Cambrian age, 15-
26
and rock strata, 115
skeletons, 68-69, 116
collection of, as hobby, 7-9
coral, 21
dating of, 7-9
dinosaur, 70-86
in England, 91
eggs of *Protoceratops,* 99
explanation of, 2-3
findings
of Ice Age, 187
identification of, 169
and theory of evolution, 4ʳ